ABOUT THE

Jessica Bell is an Australian
coach, novelist, poet, and s
who lives in Athens, Greece. I ...tion to her novels, her poetry collections (including *Fabric*, which was nominated for the Goodreads Readers Choice Awards in 2012), and her bestselling pocket writing guides ("Writing in a Nutshell" series), she has published a variety of works online and in literary journals and anthologies, including *Writer's Digest* and Australia's *Cordite Review*. Additionally, she is the Co-Founder and Publishing Editor of *Vine Leaves Literary Journal*, and coordinates a variety of writing workshops worldwide.

Visit her website: *jessicabellauthor.com*

ALSO BY JESSICA BELL

Novels
White Lady
Bitter Like Orange Peel
The Book
String Bridge

Short Fiction & Poetry
She: a short story in verse
Muted: a short story in verse
The Hum of Sin Against Skin
Fabric
Twisted Velvet Chains

Writing in a Nutshell Series
Polish Your Fiction: A Quick & Easy Self-Editing Guide
(Book 5)

Writing in a Nutshell:
Writing Workshops to Improve Your Craft
(Book 4—Books 1, 2, and 3 combined with bonus material)

The Six Senses in a Nutshell:
Demonstrated Transitions from Bleak to Bold Narrative (Book 3)

Adverbs & Clichés in a Nutshell:
Demonstrated Subversions of Adverbs & Clichés Into Gourmet Imagery
(Book 2)

Show & Tell in a Nutshell:
Demonstrated Transitions from Telling to Showing (Book 1)

Compiled & Edited
The Best of Vine Leaves Literary Journal 2014
The Best of Vine Leaves Literary Journal 2013
The Best of Vine Leaves Literary Journal 2012
Indiestructible: Inspiring Stories from the Publishing Jungle

SELF-PUBLISH YOUR BOOK
A Quick & Easy Step-by-Step Guide

ISBN-10: 0994283741
ISBN-13: 978-0-9942837-4-0

Published by Vine Leaves Press, 2015
Melbourne, Victoria, Australia | Athens, Attica, Greece

National Library of Australia Cataloguing-in-Publication entry
Creator: Bell, Jessica Carmen, author.
Title: Self-publish your book : a quick & easy step-by-step guide / Jessica Bell.
ISBN: 9780994283740 (paperback)
Subjects: Self-publishing—Handbooks, manuals, etc.
Publishers and publishing.
Dewey Number: 070.593

Cover and interior design by Jessica Bell

SELF-PUBLISH YOUR BOOK

A Quick & Easy Step-by-Step Guide

jessica bell

Vine Leaves Press
Melbourne, Victoria, Australia | Athens, Attica, Greece

To all writers out there who need something to be easy for once.

CONTENTS

i

INTRODUCTION

G'day! It's Jessica again with another Nutshell book. If you're new to the "Writing in a Nutshell" series, welcome! Hopefully this book will make your life a little easier, and save you precious time and money. Before I get down to business, I'd like first to establish whether this book is for you.

This book is for you if your book is ready for publication and you can answer "true" to one or more of the following statements:

- *I have never self-published before and have no idea what I'm doing.*
- *I have never self-published before, don't want to spend*

any money doing so, but still want to end up with a quality product.

- *I have never self-published before and I'm looking for the quickest, most hassle-free, and cheapest way to do so.*
- *I have only self-published with a vanity publisher before and am not happy with their service.*
- *I have self-published before, but I have always hired freelancers to do all the work and need some guidance to take control and save money.*
- *I have self-published before, but I am not happy with the quality of my work and need some help to make it better this time.*
- *I have self-published before, but it took me so long, and cost me so much money—I need help getting organized to help manage my time.*

Now, you may also be wondering, why another book on self-publishing? Isn't the market saturated with these types of books already? And what can I tell you that another book can't? Well, you may have a point, but the beauty of my Nutshell books is that they do not overwhelm you with all the information available—they tell you specifically what you need to know, without all the faff, and follow one particular method.

If you're the type of person, like me, who needs to tick things off a list to feel organized, then you're reading the right book. This self-publishing guide offers you a step-by-step, foolproof, cost-efficient, time-efficient, extremely easy-to-follow process for making your books available for sale. Sometimes I may cut in very briefly with an alternative to what I'm proposing, but I promise the interruption will be short and to the point, and most likely lead you to another resource in case you'd like to know more.

You'll notice that there are black and white picture aids at the back of the book which will help you to better understand my instructions. Whenever a picture aid is necessary, I will tell you to refer to it. If you would like to see these pictures in colour (and much bigger!), you can download the PDF file from ***jessicabellauthor.com/self-publish-your-book-templates.html***. You will be prompted to enter this password to gain access: JCB260202.

So ... are you ready to get started?

ii

COMPUTER SOFTWARE NEEDED

DIY Self-Publishing cannot be DIY if you don't have specific software to help you out. If you don't already have the following software, I suggest you get it, especially if you intend to self-publish more books completely on your own.

You are going to need the following software to fulfil every step in this book:

1. Microsoft Word (free for a 30-day trial) to prepare your manuscript and paperback interior layout;
2. Adobe Photoshop (free for a 30-day trial) to design your cover;

3. Adobe Acrobat Pro (free for a 30-day trial), which is a PDF creator and editor for your printable cover and interior;
4. Notepad++ (free for life) to format your eBook; and
5. Calibre (free for life) to convert your eBook into a retail-ready file.

In addition to the above, I use InDesign to do the paperback interior layout, but you can also format paperbacks efficiently and professionally in Microsoft Word (which is what I used to do in the beginning), so for the sake of making your life easier, I'm not going to refer to InDesign at all in this book. Also, please note that I am a PC user, so any computer commands will refer to those on a PC. For Mac commands, a simple Internet search will help you out if you don't already know the equivalents.

Let me tell you a few things about the software above and why I've chosen these programs for you. They are compatible with all computers and the other software, so I strongly suggest you do not skimp on alternative programs like Open Office, or use Pages (for Mac), for example. You could end up with extraordinarily frustrating technical problems down the line. I won't go into details, so you're just going to have to trust me on that. I've been doing this for a long time and have heard many horror stories about formatting that would have been avoided had the authors been using standard software.

A small word of caution: not every person is going to own the same version of the software used in this book. If you already own the software I recommend, you may have older versions than I do. If you don't already own the software, you are going to end up with newer versions than I have. Because this book is extremely specific with its instructions, you are bound to come across a few steps that do not match 100% to what you see on your computer at home. This is unavoidable and I urge you not to fret. If something looks different to how I show it, and you can't seem to find something, simply click F1 on your keyboard for *Help*. And you also have Google. I learnt everything I know about self-publishing from the Internet and through a lot of trial and error. If you have a question, the answer is most definitely somewhere in cyberspace.

1

PREPARE YOUR MANUSCRIPT IN MICROSOFT WORD

You may think your manuscript is fine until you start commanding Word to do specific tasks and strange things begin happening. For example, if you have used tabs or spaces for the start of your paragraphs, instead of proper indents, you're going to face formatting problems later on. For example, your paragraph indents may not be aligned properly.

Note: This section is not going to tell you how to edit your manuscript. Your book should be edited and ready for publication. For information on self-editing, please refer to Book #5 in this series, *Polish Your Fiction: A Quick & Easy Self-Editing Guide*.

MANUSCRIPT PREPARATION STEP-BY-STEP:

1. Make a copy of your manuscript in case you make an irreversible mistake.

2. Show all formatting (Ctrl + Shift + 8). You will now see all the formatting marks, such as paragraph breaks, tabs, and spaces.

3. Firstly, remove any instances of double spaces after full stops. You may have been taught this in school, but it is frowned upon nowadays. To do this:

- *Select All* (Ctrl + A).
- Open the *Find and Replace* dialog box (Ctrl + H).
- Type in two spaces in the *Find* field and one space in the *Replace* field.
- Click *Replace All.*

Also, for some reason—and it happens to me too—you end up with an extra useless space at the end of paragraphs. It's a good idea to clean this up. All you have to do is replace *.[space]^p* with *.^p* and they will disappear.

Note: Do not literally type *[space]*; it means to press the space bar.

4. Find out what you have done at the beginning of new paragraphs. If there are tabs (or spaces) instead of indents:

- *Select All* (Ctrl + A)

- Open the *Find and Replace* dialogue box (Ctrl + H).
- Place your cursor in the *Find* field and then click *More* (at the bottom left).
- Now click *Special* and select *Tab Character*.
- Leave the *Replace* field blank and click *Replace All*.

If you've used spaces, just type the amount of spaces you've used into the *Find* field. If the amount of space you've used is inconsistent, you'll have to do this a few times.

5. Now all your indents will be gone, but you will fix this now. (Refer to Pic. 1a on page 90 for visual.)

- Make sure your entire content is still selected. If it's not, *Select All* again.
- Open the *Paragraph* group box located in the *Home* tab.
- In the *Indentation* section, select *First line* under *Special*.
- Now under *By*, type in *0.2*. (If your Word is set to centimetres rather than inches, type in *0.6*.)
- Make sure *Left* and *Right* are set to *0*. (While you're in there, make sure in the *Spacing* section your *Before* and *After* are set to *0*, and *Line spacing* is set to *Single*.)
- Now click *OK*.

Your indents are now back and formatted properly.

6. If you have used any automatic numbering or bullet points, disable them and insert your numbers and lists

manually. Pain in the butt? Maybe, but it will save you a headache later on as all automatic formatting will disappear when it's time to format your eBook. I won't go into that until later on, so please take my word for it.

To disable your automatic numbering and bulleting:

- Click the *Microsoft Office Button* (top left of your screen) and then click *Word Options* (bottom right of dialog box).
- Click *Proofing*.
- Click *AutoCorrect Options*, and then click the *AutoFormat As You Type* tab.
- Under *Apply as you type*, clear the *Automatic bulleted lists* tick box and/or the *Automatic numbered lists* tick box.

7. If you have used italics at all, please make sure only the word or sentence is italicized. What I mean by that is, the spaces, full stops, and/or paragraph marks before and after the italicized section should be completely free of that formatting. Again this has to do with saving you a headache later when formatting your eBook. The same goes for bolding and underlining.

Tips:

1. 0.2 inches (0.6 cm) is an ideal indent size for both paperback and eBook.
2. It's customary *not* to indent the first line of a new chapter or section. Paragraphs should only be indented if there is another paragraph preceding it. To remove the indent from the very first line of a new chapter or

section, go to the start of each chapter or section and place the cursor at the beginning of the first paragraph. Follow the procedure on how to set an indent, but select *None* instead of *First line*. Do the same for your chapter headings because they will have been indented as well.
3. Please do not use line spaces to separate paragraphs in fiction. It's common for nonfiction, but in fiction it just wastes space, especially when you have a lot of dialogue together, as each utterance generally starts on a new line.

Note: If you feel you need more guidance for preparing your manuscript please refer to "Section 2.2 Typographical Considerations" in *Polish Your Fiction: A Quick & Easy Self-Editing Guide*.

2

DESIGN YOUR EBOOK COVER

I know what you're thinking: isn't this a little premature? I don't even have the interior of my book done yet—and what about the paperback cover?

Don't stress. You're doing the eBook cover now for a very good reason. You need to know what fonts you are going to use on the cover so that you can use the same fonts inside the book for the title page and your chapter headings. Matching the look of the interior with the cover will leave you with a professional-looking quality product.

I design book covers professionally, and I do all sorts of

weird and wonderful tricks which, unfortunately, I'm not going to be able to teach you. To teach you these things would mean giving you a fully-fledged tutorial on how to use Adobe Photoshop and gifting you with my experience. And regardless, I'm sure that's not what you want out of reading this book. You want quick and easy, right?

So what I'm going to do is offer you tips on how to make a very simple yet striking cover, and give you an easy-to-use Adobe Photoshop template from which you can start and tweak to your heart's content.

Note: I use Adobe Photoshop CS4, but you may decide to download the latest version. I want you to know that this should not cause you any problems when trying to follow my instructions in this book as the program interface does not significantly change. But there will be very slight differences. If you get stuck, press F1 for *Help*.

Before I move on with the step-by-step procedure, I'd like to explain a few things so you can better understand what will make a striking cover regardless of how simple a design it is.

- Firstly, download the eBook Cover Template from ***jessicabellauthor.com/self-publish-your-book-templates.html*** (remember to enter this password to gain access: JCB260202) so that I can explain the elements to you while you're looking at it.
- Save the .psd file to your desired location and open it.

- Click *File* and then *Save As*, to save it as your own book cover with a different file name. (You do not want to alter the template. If you make a mistake that is irreversible you will have to download it again and start from scratch.)
- Open the template in Adobe Photoshop. (A message might come up saying that fonts are missing. Ignore this for now as we will install these fonts soon.)

Now that you have the template open, let's break down what you see.

1. The title is very big. So is the author name. In the age of online shopping, you want your title and name still to be readable when the cover image is seen at thumbnail size. On your left you should see a vertical tool bar. If not, go to *Window* and select *Tools* (right at the bottom of the dropdown menu) and the vertical tool bar will pop up. Look for the little magnifying glass. Click it. Then at the top left of your screen, you will see a magnifying glass with a plus sign and a magnifying glass with a minus sign. Click the magnifying glass with the minus sign until the cover becomes the size of a thumbnail image on Amazon. (If your version of Photoshop doesn't have the magnifying glass with the minus sign, then you can zoom out by going to *View* (top tool bar) and selecting *Zoom Out*.) Can you still read the title and the author name? Yes. This is what you need.

2. Magnify the cover back to its original size. What do you notice about the text? It uses colours that are already present in the cover image. To be safe rather than sorry, I advise you make sure you do not add any colours that aren't already there. Not only do you risk a really ugly colour clash, but you do not want to over-stimulate and confuse the brain of the person looking at it. Just like your story needs to flow and transition smoothly from one sentence and paragraph to the next, so too does the design of your cover. Less is more. Always.

3. What do you notice about the image? There is lots and lots of space. Space is vital for the eye to be attracted to it. If there is too much going on in the image, not only will you struggle to place your title and author name, but it will look too cluttered. People won't know what to focus on. Think of it this way: when there are too many characters introduced at the beginning of a book, not only do you not grasp who is who, but you might get so confused that you stop reading it. The same applies to cover design. There needs to be a clear focus for it to make sense and to hook your reader.

4. The fonts I have used are classic fonts which will translate well for a wide variety of genres. The title and author name use Trajan Pro, and the teaser text is Adobe Garamond Pro (which is also the font I'll advise you to use for your interior). I am a strong advocate for classic fonts, especially when you are just starting out as there is very little room for error. You can download these fonts from ***jessicabellauthor.com/self-publish-***

your-book-templates.html (remember to enter this password to gain access: JCB260202).

To install the fonts go to *Control Panel*, click on *Appearance and Personalization*, open the *Fonts* folder, and drag and drop all the files into it. They'll start installing immediately. (On some systems these may be labelled differently. The key is to find your *Fonts* folder.)

For a fabulous array of fonts by genre, however, you might like to take a look at this post by Creative Indie: ***creativindie.com/300-fool-proof-fonts-to-use-for-your-book-cover-design-an-epic-list-of-best-fonts-per-genre***. Many fonts are also available for free download. Just Google *Free Fonts*.

5. There is a quarter of an inch of space (0.635 cm) around the margins that is free of text. This is intentional. Even though this is an eBook cover and will not require a bleed (trimming space for the printer), we are going to transfer this design over to your paperback template later on, which *will* require a bleed. So it's best to be prepared.

Right ... let's get cracking.

EBOOK COVER DESIGN STEP-BY-STEP:

1. Find an image that best represents your book. (Do not use the one in the template. Though I have permission to use it, you do not unless you purchase it, and you could get into trouble.) You can find creative commons (copyright-free images) on Flickr: ***flickr.com/creativecommons/***, or a fabulous list of free stock photo sites here: ***bootstrapbay.com/blog/free-stock-photos***.

You can also purchase photos from a stock photo site like Shutterstock.com. This is my favourite because their subscription plans are very affordable and apparently the range of choice is the largest available (over nine million photos).

2. Once you have an image that you're happy with (remember, lots of space!), open the template you saved as your own cover. Make sure the layers panel is open. To open the layers panel, press the F7 key. The layers panel should pop up at the right of your screen. (Refer to Pic. 2a on page 91 for visual.)

See the layer that is highlighted? That's the image that is currently a part of the design. You need to remove that. To remove it, drag and drop it onto the little rubbish bin that is located at the bottom right of the layers panel. You will now see what is represented in Pic. 2b on page 92.

3. You are now going to insert your own image. Make sure the *Background* layer in the layers panel is blue so that the image we insert will be placed below the text. If the *Background* layer isn't blue, all you need to do is click on it once. Go to *File* and select *Place* (or *Place Embedded* in some versions.) (Refer to Pic. 2c on page 93 for visual.)

A dialog box will pop up for you to insert a file from your computer. Locate the image you want to use and click *Place*.

Now click the little *Maintain Aspect Ratio* button (circled in red in Pic. 2d in the PDF you downloaded) and drag the edges of the image until it covers the whole Background area and is placed how you like it. (Refer to Pic. 2d on page 94 for visual.)

Note: To remove *Maintain Aspect Ratio* just click the same button again.

4. Now before we work on the text, you need to make sure you don't place any text beyond the bleed line so, when the time comes, you can transfer this design over to your paperback cover with ease. To do this, you need to place some guide lines. It's very easy.

- First, if you don't see a ruler at the top of your screen, go to *View* and then select *Rulers*. You will now see a ruler across the top edge and along the left edge.

- Place your cursor over the ruler at the top of your screen, click, hold, and drag. You will see a horizontal line move with your cursor. Place that line a quarter of an inch (0.7 cm) below the top of the image.
- Now do the same thing, but drag the line all the way to the bottom of the image. Place it a quarter of an inch (0.7 cm) above the bottom of the image.
- Now place your cursor over the ruler at the left of your screen. Drag and drop the lines, one at the left and one at the right, a quarter of an inch (0.7 cm) in from the edges. (Refer to Pic. 2e on page 95 for visual.)

Tip: To remove a guide line, hover your cursor over it and press Ctrl. You will notice that your cursor changes appearance. Click on your guide line and drag it back up to the ruler and it will disappear.

5. Now let's fix your title.

Press T on your keyboard. You will notice that the T in the vertical tool bar to the left is now highlighted. Now click your cursor on YOUR TITLE. The text box it is in will now show up. Press Ctrl + A to select all the text and choose your desired font. (Refer to Pic. 2f on page 96 for visual.)

Keep the text selected and start typing in your book title. If it's too long for the current size of the text box, adjust the size of the text box by dragging it down from the bottom right corner, and/or adjust the size of the actual text by typing in the size you want. (Refer to Pic. 2g on page 97 for visual.) Note that you can have different words as different sizes, too. You just need to select that one word for which you want to change the size.

You will have to play around a bit to get it right depending on how long or short your title is. If you have reduced or enlarged the size of the font considerably, you may also want to alter the space between the letters and/or the words. To do this, select the text again, open the *Character* panel and adjust the numbers until the title looks the way you want it to. (Refer to Pic. 2g on page 97 for visual.) If you can't see the *Character* panel like in the image, go to *Window* (top tool bar) and select *Character* to make it pop up.

Now choose the colour you want your title to be. Remember earlier how I advised you to choose a colour that's already in your image? Let me tell (and show) you how to do that. First, *Select* the entire title (Ctrl + A) again. Then ... (Refer to Pic. 2h on page 98 for visual.)

Step 1 in Pic. 2h: Click on this to bring up the colour dialog box.
Step 2 in Pic. 2h: Click on this icon (Eyedropper tool).
Step 3 in Pic. 2h: Click the Eyedropper anywhere on the image that has the colour you want to use. You will notice that your text changes the same colour instantly.
Step 4 in Pic. 2h: Click *OK* in the colour dialog box.

Follow the same procedure for your author name and teaser text.

6. To move the position of any text on your cover, click on the layer in the layers panel so it turns blue, then press V on your keyboard. You will notice that the arrow at the very top of the vertical tool bar is now highlighted. You can now either use your mouse to move the text, or the arrows on your keyboard.

Refer to Pic. 2i on page 99 to see my completed cover using the template.

Now that you're done with your front cover, note down the names of the fonts you have used so you don't need to go back in and check while doing your book layout. You're also not going to bother saving this cover as a .jpeg just yet. You could, but it's not necessary. For now, just save it as a .psd and back it up.

3

PREPARE YOUR FRONT/BACK MATTER AND BLURB

I've said a lot about front/back matter and blurbs in *Polish Your Fiction: A Quick & Easy Self-Editing Guide*, but in that book I talk about preparing them editorially. Here I will talk about them from a slightly different perspective, so please don't skip this section.

FRONT/BACK MATTER AND BLURB ORGANIZATION STEP-BY-STEP:

FRONT MATTER

Front matter is subjective and varies from book to book, but I'm going to advise you based on what I would do.

The order isn't set in stone, but it's what I think looks best in a paperback.

1. Praise for *Title of Book*

The amount of praise is going to differ depending on the trim size of your book, and the type and size of the font used. So if you intend to put a "Praise" section in the front matter, make sure you collect enough. You can always trim the quotes down too. If you don't have any quotes, or don't want to get quotes from authors or media to put here, don't worry about it. Just start with the next step.

Tip: Here's a great article on how to get quotes for the cover of your novel on AbsoluteWrite.com (an excellent forum for writers): ***absolutewrite.com/novels/get_great_quotes.htm***

2. About the Author

A short biography. This speaks for itself really. Many authors put this section in the back, but I think it looks nice at the front in a paperback. (It's different for an eBook, however, which I will talk about later.) Just write something short and sweet, and make sure you include your website URL. Don't include the *http://www*, though, as it looks messy. For example, instead of *http://www.jessicabellauthor.com*, just write *jessicabellauthor.com*.

3. Also by *Author Name*

List all other books you've written under category headings, i.e. "Fiction", "Nonfiction", "Poetry". If you haven't published before, ignore this.

4. Title Page

Your title and author name. Centred and in a large font size preferably. If you have a publisher name you can also put this here. If you look at the title page of this book you'll see how the publisher name is located at the bottom of the page along with its location.

5. Imprint Page (a.k.a. Credit Page, Copyright Page, or Title Page Verso)

The information on this page varies with different publishers and authors, but here is a simple template for you with all the necessary information (replace the bold text with your own):

STAR LIGHT
Copyright © **2015 Jessica Bell**
All rights reserved.

Published by **Vine Leaves Press 2015**
Melbourne, Victoria, Australia

No parts of this publication may be reproduced, stored in a retrieval system, or transmitted in any form or by any means, electronic, mechanical, photocopying, recording, or otherwise, without the prior written permission of the copyright owner.

This book is sold subject to the condition that it shall not, by way of trade or otherwise, be lent, resold, hired out, or otherwise circulated without the publisher's prior consent in any form of binding or cover other than that in which it is published and without a similar condition including this condition being imposed on the subsequent purchaser. Under no circumstances may any part of this book be photocopied for resale.

This is a work of fiction. Any similarity between the characters and situations within its pages and places or persons, living or dead, is unintentional and co-incidental. *[Remove this bit if your book is nonfiction. If it's a memoir, you may like to insert: Some names and identifying details have been changed to protect the privacy of individuals.]*

Cover photography from **Shutterstock.com**
[Insert additional credits here, if applicable, such as permission to reprint copyrighted material.]

Note: You'll notice that there is no ISBN included here. I'll explain why. As a first-time self-publisher, it's really not necessary to buy your own ISBNs, as the distributors to which you are going to upload your book will provide one for you. And, because you haven't uploaded anything yet, you're not going to know what it is. That's okay. You don't need it. The distributor will include the assigned ISBN in the barcode on the back cover (which they will also provide). So I advise, in order to get your self-publishing feet wet with the least amount of hassle possible, just to ignore this side of business for now. There are a lot of for and against arguments about buying your own ISBNs. It's actually quite a discussion topic amongst self-published authors, so once you've published your first book, and begin to feel comfortable with the process, you can explore the ISBN issue further if you like. But for now, all you need to think is: *ISBNs and barcodes? All sorted.* However, if you would like to purchase your own ISBNs, I'll give you some information about that in Section 7.

6. Dedication

This can be something as simple as *For John*, or it could be a little more detailed and include a reason why. Some people include quotes from other authors that are symbolically relevant to their story. Whatever you do choose to put here, make sure it is centred and the only thing on the page. It's special.

Note: If your book is nonfiction or short stories it will also need a TOC (Table of Contents) in the front of the paperback. Take a look at the front matter of this book for an example.

END MATTER

7. There are a lot of things you can include in the back of your book. Here are some of the popular ones:

- Acknowledgements
- A suggestion to sign up to your author newsletter
- A call to connect with you on your website or other social media platforms
- A call to post a review
- Adverts for your backlist or upcoming titles
- Sample excerpts from your forthcoming titles
- An author interview
- Book club discussion questions

There is no standard way to set any of these things out. Just be creative and do what feels right for you. However, if you're writing nonfiction, there are more rigid rules and other sections you might like to consider adding. If you are writing nonfiction, check out this article: ***bookbaby.com/2013/11/between-the-covers-of-your-nonfiction-book/***

8. Back Cover Blurb

Write it now. Let it sit. Rewrite it. Let it sit. Have friends read it. Let it sit. Give it time to mature. Proofread it. Proofread it again. Then it will be perfect by the time you are ready to put it on your back cover. There is always something that won't feel right with it, and you will always be given conflicting opinions on it. For me this is the hardest part of this process, so be sure to write it early so you have the chance to make it as perfect as possible. It is after all, the second thing (after the front cover) that potential buyers look at. So please don't rush it!

4

FORMAT YOUR PAPERBACK INTERIOR

I'm going to assume you know the basics of Microsoft Word as this is the most common word processing program, so my instructions regarding the mechanics of this program's tools are not going to be as in-depth as they were for Adobe Photoshop. If there is anything you don't understand in this section, there are plenty of free online tutorials you can access. The following free tutorials are particularly cool and easy to grasp: ***gcflearnfree.org/office***.

Another thing to note: the trim size of this template is 5 x 8 inches (12.7 x 20.32 cm). This is also the trim size of the eBook cover, and will be the trim size of your paperback cover. I have chosen this trim size for the following reasons:

- It's a typical trade paperback size.
- It's not too small and it's not too big. I think it's the most comfortable size to hold when reading.
- All print-on-demand (POD) companies offer this trim size with both white and cream paper.

Note: If you want to change the trim size of the template, all you have to do is go to *Page Layout* > *Page Setup* > *Size* and select your size of choice. If you want to read about different trim sizes for various types of books, you can do so here: ***thebookdesigner.com/2010/09/self-publishing-basics-how-to-pick-the-size-of-your-book/***

The margins I have set up in the template should stay the same. Do not change these. These margins are compatible with every POD company out there and will not cause you any problems. I have mirrored the pages and made the outer edges a little wider than the industry standard. The standard 0.5 inch (1.27 cm) margins all around are way too narrow in my opinion, and the text ends up way too close to the spine of the book, which is awkward to read. Trust me, I've been through this.

Once you download the template (see below), you'll notice that it doesn't contain a header. Headers are not necessary and many traditionally published books do not use headers either. Having a header on each page is not going to determine whether your book is professionally formatted. It's simply a matter of style and choice. I have purposely left them out because, again, it's a bit of a learning curve setting them up. Even if I included them in the template, you would still have to learn how to use tools that might make your head spin. My advice is not to bother. If you do want headers, however, you can find a tutorial on how to set them up here: ***gcflearnfree.org/office***.

My instructions on formatting the paperback interior are not fancy. You will end up with a simple, clean, and classy paperback. And really, that is all you need, especially if you're just starting out.

PAPERBACK INTERIOR LAYOUT STEP-BY-STEP:

1. Download the Paperback Interior Template from: ***jessicabellauthor.com/self-publish-your-book-templates.html*** (remember the password to gain access: JCB260202). Save the .doc file to your desired location and open it. Click *File* and then *Save As* to save it as your own book interior with a different file name.

Note: The default language of the template is set to American English. If you'd like to change this, go to the *Review* tab and then click *Set Language* in the *Proofing* group.

2. If you haven't already downloaded the Adobe

Garamond Pro font and you'd like to use it, you can download that from the same link too. (I highly recommend this font. It's easy on the eye, looks professional and classy, isn't too thick or thin. For me, it's the perfect font to use for the interior of a paperback. To install the font, go to *Control Panel*, click on *Appearance and Personalization*, open the *Fonts* folder, and drag and drop the four Adobe Garamond Pro files into it. They'll start installing immediately. If you can't see the same thing as me, try to locate the *Fonts* folder.

3. Open your paperback interior template and your manuscript. Zoom out so that the template is visible as a whole page on your screen. Copy the entire contents of your manuscript and paste it into your template. Now *Select All* (Ctrl + A), change the font to Adobe Garamond Pro, 11.5 point, with 0.9 leading, and justify the text. (Refer to Pic. 4a on page 100 for visual.)

Note: If you'd prefer your font to be larger and there to be more space between lines, adjust accordingly.

4. Arrange the front matter as follows and be sure to separate each one with a *Page Break*. (Put your cursor at the end of the last word on each page and go to the *Insert* tab, *Pages* group, and click *Page Break*):

Page 1: Praise (or About the Author)
Page 2: Blank
Page 3: Also by [Author Name]

Page 4: Credits Page (Imprint Information)
Page 5: Title Page
Page 6: Blank
Page 7: Dedication
Page 8: Blank
Page 9: Start first chapter

I usually make the font size of front matter a lot smaller than the main body. You will notice the same thing in traditionally published books too. My size of choice for the "Praise", "About the Author", and "Also by [Author Name]" sections is 10 pt, and the size for the "Credits Page" is either 8pt or 9pt.

Don't worry about the page numbers showing on any of the front matter at the moment. We will fix that later.

5. Make sure the font of your chapter headings is the same as the title on your cover and that they are centred. You don't *have* to do this, but I highly recommend it. It has to do with visual aesthetics and continuity, which gives your product a professional look. Making the text size bigger is also advised. Choose whatever size you think looks best.

Most professionals would advise you to create *Styles* for your headings so that in the event that you wanted to change the way they looked, you could change them all at once. Setting up *Styles*, however, is a bit of a learning curve, so if you aren't in the mood, or don't have time, just make sure you know exactly how you want your headings to look before fixing them! If you do want to learn about setting up *Styles*, you can find a tutorial at the ***gcflearnfree.org/office*** link I mentioned earlier.

6. Make sure the beginning of each chapter starts on a new page. Do **not** use the *Enter* key to get it there. Insert a *Page Break*. If you'd like your chapters to start midway down the page, the typical way to do this would be to create *Sections*. Again, this is complicated. Forget about that. After your page break, just press *Enter* an equal amount of times at the beginning of each chapter. Professional formatters are going to be screaming at me for telling you this. In fact, I'm kinda screaming at myself. But you know what? You're going to end up with the same result by doing this the lazy way, so why should I rob you of that knowledge? And seeing as we won't be using the Word document for your eBook, it makes no difference.

7. Arrange each section of your back matter on a new page, using a *Page Break*.

(The following step is for those who would like to insert images.)

8. To insert images, do not copy and paste as they will diminish in quality.

Note: Make sure all your images are print-ready. They need to be at least 300 DPI, and scaled to size. If you are new to this, please check out these articles for help: ***booksat.scarlettrugers.com/bookcoverdesign/standard-size-of-a-book-and-understanding-image-size-and-resolution/*** and ***blog.klmimages.com/2010/09/resolution-overview/***

- Place your cursor where you want your image to go.
- Go to the *Insert* tab and click *Picture* in the *Illustrations* group.
- Locate your desired picture and click *Insert.*
- Right-click on the inserted picture and select *Format Picture* (or *Size*, or *Size and Position*, if either of those options are available to you).
- Click on the *Size* tab (if you chose *Format Picture*).
- Tick the boxes next to *Lock aspect ratio* and *Relative to original picture size.*
- Adjust to desired percentage next to *Height* or *Width*. You only need to alter one because you've ticked *Lock aspect ratio*. (Refer to Pic. 4b on page 101 for visual.)

Note: Unfortunately, on earlier versions of Word you can't see the image changing size while you do this, so it may take a few tries before you get it how you want.

Tip: If you want to move the position of the picture, you can simply drag and drop.

5

PROOFREAD YOUR FORMATTED PAGES

I know you've probably proofread your work a million times and are utterly sick of it, but this step is important because we are now checking for more than textual errors: we're also checking for layout errors.

PROOFREAD YOUR FORMATTED PAGES STEP-BY-STEP:

1. Print out your formatted pages in *Landscape* mode with two book pages per one printed page so it is a similar size as an actual book. The way to do this will differ depending on your printer, so I'm afraid you're going to have to figure this bit out for yourself.

2. Read it through from beginning to end, red pen in hand, and look for the following:

a. typographical errors (you'll be surprised how many you didn't catch before!)
b. inconsistent spacing between lines and words
c. too many hyphenated words in the right margins
d. single words hanging at the end of paragraphs
e. chapter headings that are inconsistent in appearance or numbering
f. page breaks that are not in the right place.

3. Now implement your corrections into the paperback layout .doc. Once you're done with that, make a copy of the file and name it *TITLE_eBook*. You will soon use this file to create your eBook. Your interior layout is probably in perfect shape by now, but if you're in doubt, ask a trusted friend to have a read through it before you move on.

4. Open your paperback layout .doc again and:

- Go to *Word Options*. (Refer to Pic. 5a on page 102 for visual.)
- Go to *Save* and select *Embed fonts*, click *OK*. Close the document. (Refer to Pic. 5b on page 103 for visual.)

Your paperback interior is now ready for the final touches.

6

SAVE YOUR INTERIOR LAYOUT AS A PRINT-READY PDF

Time to warm up the engines of Adobe Acrobat Pro. Unfortunately, the simple Adobe Reader does not have all the functions you need, so you're going to have to embrace Adobe Acrobat Pro. And trust me, as time goes by, and you become more experienced in publishing, you are going to thank your lucky stars that you have this program.

What we are going to do in this section is very simple, but it's essential to have this program because you are also going to need it when the time comes to export your paperback cover as well. All POD companies accept PDFs, so I strongly believe it's in your best interests to have the ability to create PDF documents.

You'll find it also comes in handy for a lot of other things related to your self-publishing business in the future. Not only do POD companies prefer the PDF format for your print-ready files, but so do a lot of real-life human reviewers! Strange, I know. I would much prefer a proper eBook file to transfer to my eReader than read from a PDF, but as experience shows, when I ask what format a reviewer would like my book in, 90% of them ask for a PDF.

SAVE AS A PDF STEP-BY-STEP:

1. Open Adobe Acrobat Pro. Click on *File*, select *Open*, select *All Files* in the dialog box that opens up, and select your edited paperback layout document (not the original template). Once it converts to PDF, save as *TITLE_for_print* in your desired location. (Refer to Pic. 6a on page 104 for visual.)

Note: In newer versions of Word you can save your document as an Adobe PDF from *Save As*. If you prefer to do it this way, go for it. It should automatically open up in Adobe Acrobat Pro if you have that set as the default PDF viewer. If not, you're going to have to open it within the program.

2. Remove page numbers from the desired pages.

- Open your *TITLE_for_print* PDF.
- Go to *View* > *Page Display* > *Two-Up* (or *Two Page View* in some versions). (Refer to Pic. 6b on page 105 for visual.)
- Go to *Tools* > *Advanced Editing* > *Touch-Up Text Tool* (or *Tools* > *Edit PDF* > *Edit* in some versions). (Refer to Pic. 6c on page 106 for visual.)
- Place the cursor in front of the page numbers you want to delete and hit the delete key.

3. Save the file. You now have a print-ready PDF for upload to any POD company that exists.

7

REGISTER WITH DESIRED RETAILERS/DISTRIBUTORS

The reason we are registering with distributors before designing your paperback cover is because there are a few factors which are going to determine the width of your book spine.

Once you register with your POD distributor of choice, you will be able to enter your trim size (the size and shape of your book), page count, and paper colour into their system, and the distributor will create a cover template for you with the necessary spine width according to their specifications.

Before we get you registering, I'd like first to talk about

what I believe are your best options. I have used every distributor I'm going to recommend, so I can tell you about these from firsthand experience.

OPTION ONE

You want to spend zero money and can put up with a little bit of uncomplicated, but sometimes time-consuming hassle (especially in the long term when you need to keep track of sales reports and royalties from different places). You're not too fussed about your book only being available from the major retailers (Amazon, Barnes & Noble, Kobo, and iBooks). If this sounds like you, I advise you distribute with:

- CreateSpace for print
- Kindle Direct Publishing for Amazon Kindle
- Kobo for Kobo, and
- Draft2Digital for iBooks and Nook retailers.

Never heard of these things before? Let me break them down for you.

CreateSpace is owned by Amazon. It enables you to self-publish in print for free from anywhere in the world. The clincher is that your print book will only be available for sale at Amazon. If you want CreateSpace to distribute to other retailers, such as Barnes & Noble and Chapters Indigo, you will have to pay a fee.

Kindle Direct Publishing (KDP) is also owned

by Amazon. It enables you to publish your book electronically on Amazon for Kindle from anywhere in the world. (In case you don't know, Kindle is an eReader that is exclusive to Amazon.)

Kobo is an eBook retailer. (It is also the name of their eReading device.) They do not act as a distributor for your eBook. Uploading to Kobo means that your book will be available on Kobo only for readers to purchase from Kobo only. You can upload to Kobo from anywhere in the world without any problems.

Draft2Digital is a distributor who lists your eBook at multiple retailers. Most importantly iBooks (iTunes) and Nook (Barnes & Noble). They also distribute to Kobo and a couple of other less popular sites, but they do take a little cut from your royalties which is why I suggest uploading to Kobo separately. The reason I'm recommending you use Draft2Digital for iBooks and Nook is because these retailers do not allow you to upload your book from anywhere in the world. Well, they do ... but you might not be able to get paid because they do not accept bank accounts from all countries. Being an expat myself, I am aware of these restrictions and think you should know. If you live in the US or UK, however, you will have no problem directly uploading your books to iBooks and Nook, just like I have suggested you do at Kobo.

To register for Option One, go to the following URLs and follow their registration guidelines:

CreateSpace: ***createspace.com***
Kindle Direct Publishing: ***kdp.amazon.com***
Kobo: ***writinglife.kobobooks.com***
Draft2Digital: ***draft2digital.com*** (for iBooks and Nook + others)
or
iBooks: ***itunesconnect.apple.com***
Nook: ***nookpress.com***

OPTION TWO

As Amazon is a huge player in this industry, you will benefit from going through Kindle Direct Publishing regardless, as you will be able to retain a 70% royalty per sale from them. This is a no-brainer for me, and should be for you too.

If you're keen to spend a small set-up fee for minimal hassle in the long run, I advise you register with IngramSpark. IngramSpark doubles as a print and ePub distributor, which saves you an enormous hassle, as you can upload all your files in one place, and all your sales reports and royalties will come from the same place, too. Also, the list of retailers they distribute to is phenomenal, and even though you are going to get the majority of sales via the four main players, the more places your book is available, the better for your visibility online.

To see IngramSpark's distribution partners, visit:
www1.ingramspark.com/Portal/distribution_partner

To see the retailers to which IngramSpark distributes, visit:
www1.ingramspark.com/Portal/online_retail_partners

IngramSpark has been a lifesaver for me as I'm very busy and I prefer spending a little money for the luxury of saving some time. And it doesn't just save me uploading time. It means I don't have to compile sales reports from multiple places. Everything ends up in one place. Check out Pic. 7a on page 107 for my public endorsement!

However, there is a bit of a downside. You have to provide your own ISBNs to distribute through IngramSpark and they cost money in most countries. I know, I know, I'm sorry. But you want my opinion? If you intend to publish lots of books in the future, and would like to go the IngramSpark no-hassle route, I would buy a batch of 100 ISBNs and be done with having to worry about them for a very long time. The costs vary per country.

Note: If you choose to purchase ISBNs, you will need to assign one ISBN for the paperback and another ISBN for the ePub. So you'll need two ISBNs per book if you go this route. You will not need an ISBN for your Kindle eBook because Amazon will assign it an ASIN, which is an exclusive Amazon Kindle cataloguing number.

Here's a list of where you can purchase ISBNs:

Australia
Thorpe-Bowker: ***myidentifiers.com.au***
Prices range from $42 for a single ISBN (plus a $55 registration fee for new publishers) to $2,890 for a block of 1,000.

United Kingdom and Republic of Ireland
Neilsen: ***isbn.nielsenbook.co.uk***
Prices start from £120 (plus VAT) for the smallest block.

Canada
Library and Archives Canada: ***bac-lac.gc.ca***
Free! (The way it should be, in my opinion!)

United States
Bowker: ***isbn.org***
Prices start at $125.00 for a single number.

If you're not located in any of the above countries, you can obtain ISBNs from your respective national ISBN registration agency. A directory of ISBN agencies is available here: ***isbn-international.org***

To register for Option Two, go to the following URLs and follow their registration guidelines:

Kindle Direct Publishing: ***kdp.amazon.com***
IngramSpark: ***ingramspark.com***

If you'd like a comprehensive list of distributors, retailers, and assisted self-publishing services, as well as information about specific costs and royalty rates to compare, you might like to check out *Choosing a Self-Publishing Service* by Jim Giammatteo: ***selfpublishingadvice.org/shop/***. But if you were looking for this, you probably wouldn't be reading this book!

8

RETRIEVE YOUR PAPERBACK COVER TEMPLATE

You're going to have to get this from either CreateSpace or IngramSpark, depending on which company you've decided to go with.

RETRIEVE YOUR PAPERBACK COVER TEMPLATE FROM CREATESPACE STEP-BY-STEP:

1. Go to: ***createspace.com/Help/Book/Artwork.do***. You'll see a little box with dropdown menus to the bottom left of your screen called *Configure your Template*. (Please note this link is case sensitive.)

2. Fill it in as follows:

Interior: *Black and White*
Trim Size: *5" x 8"* (if you've chosen a different size for your book, choose that)
Number of Pages: (your page count)
Paper Colour: *Cream* (if you want white, choose White, though cream for novels is more common.)

Then click *Build Template.*

3. Click *Click here to begin download.* Save to your desired location. Extract the .zip file into the same location. The extracted content will be a folder called unzipped. Go into that and you will find both a PDF and a PNG file. We are going to use the PDF, so feel free to delete the PNG.

RETRIEVE YOUR PAPERBACK COVER TEMPLATE FROM INGRAMSPARK STEP-BY-STEP:

1. Before you can get your template, you need to enter your title information into their system. So go to your IngramSpark dashboard, click *Add a New Title* and follow the directions. It's a very clear procedure. Once you log in, you will see what to do.

You don't need to fill this in perfectly right now. You can go back to it later to be sure you have filled in your book description, categories, and key words as best you can. Just make sure the main information, such as ISBN, title, author name, trim size (5" x 8"), interior colour (Black & White), binding type (Paperback >

Perfect Bound), and page count is entered correctly. Then save it as a draft.

2. Now go to: ***www1.ingramspark.com/Tools/CoverTemplateGenerator*** (case-sensitive link) and fill in the form as follows:

13 Digit ISBN: *(Your ISBN)*
Publisher Reference Number: *(Blank)*
Trim Size: *5.000" x 8.000" (203 mm x 127 mm)*
Interior Colour and Paper: *Black & White > Cream*
Binding Type: *Paperback > Perfect Bound*
Laminate Type: *Gloss (or Matte if you like)*
Page Count: *(Your page count)*
File Type: *PDF*
Email Address: *(Your email address)*
Confirm Email Address: *(Your email address)*
Price: *(Blank)*
Currency: *(Leave as is)*
Price in Bar Code: *No*

Most of this information should automatically insert itself anyway when you type in the ISBN because you set up the title earlier.

4. You'll get an email in seconds with your PDF template attached. Download it to your desired location.

9

DESIGN YOUR PAPERBACK COVER

Now that you have your paperback template, open up Adobe Photoshop again. I'm going to use the IngramSpark template to demonstrate most of what to do as, generally, the same procedure applies. Where it differs, I will make sure you know.

DESIGN YOUR PAPERBACK COVER STEP-BY-STEP:

1. Open your paperback template. A dialog box that looks something like Pic. 9a on page 108 will pop up.

Make sure all the fields are filled in, the same as in the

image. If you're uploading to IngramSpark, make sure it says *CMYK Colour* next to *Mode*. If you're uploading to CreateSpace, make sure it says *RGB Colour*. Press *OK*.

2. Save as *TITLE_pb_cover* for now in your desired location.

3. For the IngramSpark template, create another layer for your barcode. To do this, copy and paste it in the same position by using the *Rectangular Marquee Tool*.

- Press the M on your keyboard to activate it.
- Drag the cursor around the barcode so that you can see what looks like a perforated line around it.
- Press Ctrl + C and then Ctrl + V. You will see that a new layer pops up in the layers panel.
- Rename that as *Barcode*. You can now move it to any position you like on the back cover.

(Refer to Pic. 9b on page 109 for visual.)

For CreateSpace, you don't need to do anything like this as they will insert the barcode for you after you upload your design. You will see on their template that they have included a yellow rectangle where it will appear. Unfortunately, you can't move the barcode to any other place on the cover with CreateSpace. However, if you'd like to know where it is, so that you are sure you are leaving enough space for it, and/or not covering it up with text, create another layer as described above and then just remove it when you are finished with the design.

4. Now drag horizontal and vertical guide lines so that they line up with the inside and outside of the shading around the edges and along the spine. (Remember how we did that when designing the eBook cover? If not, see **eBook cover design step-by-step**, Step 4, to remind yourself.) Here, refer to Pic. 9c on page 110 for visual. The lines I have inserted are dark blue.

5. You are now going to insert your eBook design.

- Make sure the *Background* layer in the layers panel is highlighted so that the eBook design will be placed below the barcode. If the *Background* layer isn't highlighted, all you need to do is click on it once. For CreateSpace this won't matter.
- Go to *File* and select *Place* (or *Place Embedded* in other versions).
- A dialog box will pop up for you to insert a file from your computer. Locate the Photoshop file of your eBook cover and click *Place*.
- Use your keyboard arrows to position the cover on the right side of the template so the text is within the guide lines. (If you're using the IngramSpark template, the image will overlap the edges for now. If you're using the CreateSpace template, you will only have this issue with the left side, where the spine is. Don't worry about this as we'll fix it later.)
- Click the tick in the top tool bar to place the image.

Your front cover is now inserted and should look something like Pic. 9d on page 111.

6. Now you need to cover the back cover (left side of your template) with a mirror image of your front image.

- Follow the procedure for placing an image, and choose the plain image file (the image you downloaded, not your eBook design).
- Now go to *Edit > Transform > Flip Horizontal.* (Refer to Pic. 9e on page 112 for visual.)
- Align the right side of the image to the left side of your eBook cover image so that it looks like one fluid picture.

AN ALTERNATIVE TO A MIRRORED IMAGE:

If you don't like the look of the mirrored image, you can simply insert a single block of colour on the back.

- Press U on your keyboard to activate the *Rectangle* tool.
- Place your cursor at the top left corner and draw a rectangle over the entire cover.
- To fill with colour, double-click on the coloured section in your new layer—it will be called something like *Shape 1*—and choose your desired colour. Make sure the colour doesn't clash with your front image!
- If your solid colour is placed on top of your front image, all you need to do is reposition the layer in

the layers panel (just drag and drop). In other words, the layer at the very top of your layers panel will be placed in front of all the others and the layer at the very bottom of your layers panel will be placed behind all the others.

- It's advisable to extend your front image over your spine to avoid printing inconsistencies. Print-on-demand printers aren't always 100% precise and sometimes the folds of the spine don't fold exactly where indicated on their templates. This means if an image is severely cropped right at the edge of a fold, it might overlap onto the spine by a few millimetres, which can look shoddy. But if your image covers the spine, and is extended by a quarter of an inch or so onto the back cover, you won't have this problem.

If you'd like your front image to fade into the solid colour at the back, do the following:

- In your layers panel, at the bottom, you will see some little icons.
- With your front image selected in the layers panel, click the *Add Layer Mask* icon (it has a grey background and a white circle in the middle.)
- See the white square that is linked with your front image layer? Click your cursor on that white square. Then press G on your keyboard. This will activate your *Gradient* tool.
- Now drag your cursor from the left edge of your front cover image to the right edge of your spine. See how it fades? Do this multiple times until the edge of the front image is completely blended in.

7. If you've chosen to use the mirrored image and it doesn't completely cover the left side of your template, you're going to have to fix that. For example, see how in Pic. 9f on page 113 you can still see a little bit of the template background?

Even though this is the trim area and will most likely be cut off, it's better to be safe than sorry. If the book gets printed slightly off centre (which can happen with POD on the rare occasion), you may end up with a light blue line (or a red one if you're working with the CreateSpace template) at the back edge of your book.

So use the same technique for copying the barcode to select a thin slither of the back image:

- Press M on your keyboard to activate the *Rectangular Marquee Tool.*
- Drag the cursor around the edge of the back image so that you can see what looks like a perforated line around it.
- Press Ctrl + C and then Ctrl + V. You will see that a new layer pops up in the layers panel.
- Rename that layer *Back slither* so you don't get confused about what it is.
- Now mirror that back slither with your main back image: *Edit > Transform > Flip Horizontal.*
- Use your keyboard arrows to adjust the placement as necessary.

8. Now you need to merge all these images to make them one.

- In the layers panel, click on your eBook cover layer so it is highlighted.
- Now hold down the Ctrl key and click on your back slither layer and your cover image layer (or your solid colour layer). All three layers should now be highlighted.
- Hold your cursor over one of your selected layers, right click and select *Merge Layers*. (Refer to Pic. 9g on page 114 for visual.)

The name of that layer will change once merged, so rename it if you like. I've renamed mine as *cover image*. (To rename, just double-click on the text of the layer and it will become editable.)

9. You may skip this step if you're using the CreateSpace template. If you're using the IngramSpark template, we're going to trim the edges of your cover image so that it doesn't overlap the edges into the transparent area. It's very important that you do this as IngramSpark make it very clear in their guidelines that nothing should be placed outside of the shaded areas.

- Press E to activate the *Eraser* tool.
- Choose the *Soft Round 100 Pixels* brush. (Refer to Pic. 9h on page 115 for visual.)
- Make sure your cover image layer is selected in the layers panel.

- Hold down the Shift key (it will keep your cursor moving in a straight line), and drag the cursor along each edge of your cover to erase any overlapping image. You should only erase the image up to the outer guide line. (Refer to Pic. 9i on page 116 for visual.)

10. To add text to the back of your cover:

- Press T and insert a text box where you want the text to appear.
- Copy and paste your back cover text into the text box and adjust the font type, size, and alignment to however you want it to look. You can locate these in the tool bar at the top of your screen. If you want justified text, you can change that in the paragraph panel on the right. (Refer to Pic. 9j on page 117 for visual.)
- Make sure the text is centred between the inner guide lines and does not overlap the barcode. If your text box is the size you want it, but isn't centred properly, all you have to do is press V and use your keyboard arrows (or drag it with your mouse) to move it to where you want it.

If you can't read your text properly, here are a couple of solutions:

- For dark text on a primarily light background, create an *Outer Glow*.
- For light text on a primarily dark background create a *Drop Shadow*.

How to create an *Outer Glow*:

- Double-click on your text layer.
- Select the *Outer Glow* box.
- Click *OK*. (Refer to Pic. 9k on page 118 for visual.)
- Now double-click on the actual text that reads *Outer Glow*, which will appear under your text layer.
- Play around with the *Spread* and *Size* under *Elements* until it looks the way you want it to.
- (Refer to Pic. 9l on page 119 for visual.)

How to create a *Drop Shadow*:

- Follow the same procedure for *Outer Glow*, but select *Drop Shadow* instead.
- To make sure the shadow appears evenly behind the words (rather than at an angle), under *Structure* set the *Angle* at 90 degrees. Play around with the *Spread* and *Size* until it looks the way you want it to. You may also like to set the *Distance* to 0, but the difference in appearance from the default is minimal. (Refer to Pic. 9m on page 120 for visual.)

Feel free to add any other information you'd like to the bottom left hand corner next to the barcode. I often add my publisher logo and a bit of copyright information. But it's totally up to you. I've seen others add their website URL, which I also think is a good idea. You might also like to have a look at the back of traditionally published books for ideas. (Refer to Pic. 9n on page 121 for visual.)

11. To add text to your spine, follow the general text-box procedure. Don't worry that it's not placed over your spine to begin with. Just add it horizontally to anywhere on your cover and alter the text to the way you want it to look. To rotate your text, go to *Edit* > *Transform* > *Rotate 90° CW*. (Refer to Pic. 9o on page 122 for visual.)

Move the text onto the spine. Make sure it's centred between the inner guide lines. (Refer to Pic. 9p on page 123 for visual.)

12. One more thing before you shut down Adobe Photoshop: you need to save it as a print-ready PDF.

- Make a copy of your file and save it as *TITLE_pb_cover_flat*.
- Go to *Layer* > *Flatten Image*. (Refer to Pic. 9q on page 124 for visual.)
- —Go to *File* > *Save As*.
- In the dialog box, change the name of your file to *YourISBN_cov* for IngramSpark, or keep it as is for CreateSpace. Select *Photoshop PDF* in the dropdown menu and click *Save*. If a message pops up telling you about settings being overridden, just click *OK*. (Refer to Pic. 9r on page 125 for visual.)

Note: For IngramSpark, your Interior PDF file must also be named with your ISBN before uploading, in the format *YourISBN_txt* .

- Now a *Save Adobe PDF* dialog box will pop up. In the Adobe PDF Preset field, make sure you select *PDF/X-1a:2001* and click *Save PDF*. (Refer to Pic. 9s on page 126 for visual.)

13. Now open your eBook cover in Photoshop, flatten it (*Layer > Flatten Image*.), name it *TITLE_eBook_cover_flat* and save it as a *.JPEG*. You will need a .jpeg of your eBook cover for retailers and for when you prepare your retail-ready eBook file.

10

FORMAT YOUR EBOOK INTERIOR

There are so many different techniques for creating eBook files—and I have tried almost every single one of them. There are many "easy" ways to create eBook files from a Word document, but you know what? I don't trust them, because every single time I have done that, I have run into problems. Sometimes the formatting doesn't look the way it's supposed to, sometimes the distributor rejects the file because there is something wrong with the coding that you can't see, or sometimes one of the retailers rejects it for a similar reason. So ... after many years of experimenting with different techniques, I have finally come across the best and most foolproof technique there is which will guarantee a completely clean and error-free eBook file that you can upload everywhere without a glitch.

I must bow and offer a huge thanks to Guido Henkel's *Zen of eBook Formatting*, a book which shows you step by step how to create an eBook using an HTML editor (Notepad++). Don't worry, I'm not going to make you read it! (Though I suggest you do at some point if you want to start doing more fancy things with your books.) What I'm going to do is give you a nice, clean template to work from, into which you can just copy and paste specific sections of your manuscript after a few tweaks in the Word document. In the following section, I will then tell you how to convert your HTML file into an ePub file which you will be able to upload to every single distributor and/or retailer available to you—including Kindle!

FORMAT YOUR EBOOK STEP-BY-STEP:

1. Open your file *TITLE_eBook* in Word. We need to add a few small codes to your Word .doc to make sure it all translates over to HTML without any fuss.

2. Identify and format all words in italics.

- Click Ctrl + H.
- In the *Find what* field, insert your cursor, click on *More* and then click on *Format* at the bottom of the dialog box.
- In the dropdown menu select *Font*.

- Another dialog box will pop up. In the *Font style* field, choose *Italic* and click *OK*. (Refer to Pic. 10a on page 127 for visual.)
- Now insert *<i>^&</i>* in the *Replace* field and click *OK*. (Refer to Pic. 10b on page 128 for visual.)
- All words in italics in your Word .doc will now look like this: <i>*words in italics*</i>
- Do the same for your bold text, but use *<b>^&</b>* instead of *<i>^&</i>*.

3. Replace all en-dashes and/or em-dashes with the correct HTML code to be sure they appear correctly.

- In the *Find and Replace* dialog box insert the en-dash (–), or em-dash (—), whichever one you use, into the *Find* field.
- Insert *–* (en-dash) or *—* (em-dash) into the *Replace* field and press *OK*.

4. Locate any accented letters, for example the *é* in *café*, and replace them with the correct HTML code. You can find a great list here: ***starr.net/is/type/htmlcodes.html***

5. If you have images in your manuscript, remove them. In their place, type the following:
<img src="filename.jpg"/>.
If you want your images centred, add:
<center><img src="filename.jpg"/></center> instead.

Note: Make sure you actually replace *filename* in the above with the exact name of your image file.

6. Download the *eBook_Interior_Template.html* from ***jessicabellauthor.com/self-publish-your-book-templates.html*** (password to gain access: JCB260202). Make a copy of the template and save one copy in another folder so you can keep using it for your future books.

7. Open the template in *Notepad++*, which is your HTML editing program and *Save as* the title of your book. (If you have images in your book, be sure to put all your images in the same folder as this file.)

You will see a whole lot of coding at the top, which you most likely will not understand in the slightest. Just ignore all of that. I have inserted it to make your life easy. (If you'd like to understand what it all means, read Guido Henkel's, *Zen of eBook Formatting*.)

Tip: To see what the formatting will actually look like, double-click on the HTML file in its folder to open it in your Internet browser. You can decrease the size of your browser window to that of an eReader screen to get a better idea of appearance. Please note, however, that page breaks do not show up in your browser. Also, when you make changes to the HTML file in Notepad++, you will need to click *Save* and then refresh your browser for the changes to take effect there.

8. Scroll down to where you can see *Your Title, Your Name*, and *Dedication*. From this point on, any text that is black, can be replaced. While you're there, replace

Your Title, Your Name, and *Dedication* with the correct text. Be very careful not to remove any of the coding on the left and right of the text. If even one character/symbol is removed, the formatting will be removed also. (Refer to Pic. 10c on page 129 for visual.)

9. Now scroll down a little further, where you will see *Chapter 1*. You can leave that as is if you're happy with the beginning of your chapters starting like that. I've numbered each consecutively all the way up to 25. If your chapters have titles instead of numbers, just replace the text with what you want it to be. Do not mess with what is before and after the text on this line, as it is formatted to have special qualities, such as larger font and a page break before it.

10. If you have more than 25 chapters, all you have to do is copy and paste extra segments after Chapter 25 and insert new numbers. The text you should copy and paste, looks like Pic. 10d on page 129.

Similarly, if you have fewer than 25 chapters, you can remove those that you don't need.

11. If you'd like to add a subtitle, paste your subtitle over the text that says *Your Chapter Title. Remove this whole line if you don't have one. If you'd like to use the title instead of "Chapter 1", insert it in the line above.* If you don't have any need for this, remove all the lines that look like this, including the coding before and after them. (Refer to Pic. 10e on page 129 for visual.)

12. Now replace all instances of *The first paragraph of your chapter goes here* with the first paragraph of each chapter. I have formatted this paragraph not to be indented, and to automatically turn the first line into SMALL CAPS. The number of words on the first line will change when a reader alters the font and text size on their eReading device. The formatting I have here will ensure that the words *only* on the first line of the first paragraph will be capitalized.

13. Now replace all instances of *<p>The rest of your chapter goes here.</p>* with the rest of each chapter. The codes *<p>* and *</p>* mark the opening and closing of each paragraph. I'm making you select these bits too so that they don't double up in the next step.

14. We now have to insert *<p>* and *</p>* at the beginning and end of each paragraph. Don't freak out. You don't have to do this manually.

- Select all the paragraphs in Chapter 1 (from paragraph two onwards).
- Press Ctrl + H for the *Find and Replace* dialog box to pop up.
- Make sure *Regular expression* is selected (bottom left of dialog box) and insert the following (Refer to Pic. 10f on page 130 for visual.):
  Find what: ^(.+)$
  Replace with: <p>$1</p>
- Click *Replace All.*

All your paragraphs will now have a *<p>* at the beginning and *</p>* at the end. It's necessary for these to be there so that each paragraph, from paragraph two onwards, starts on a new line and is indented. (Refer to Pic. 10g on page 131 for visual.)

Repeat Step 14 for each chapter.

15. Now complete the end matter with the relevant information using the skills you have learned in Steps 7–14. Remember, only replace text that is black.

11

EXPORT YOUR HTML (EBOOK) TO A RETAIL-READY FILE

Terms you need to know first:

.mobi: This is the name of the eBook format that Amazon uses. There is no other eBook retailer, except for Amazon, that uses this format.

.ePub: This is the name of the eBook format used for the majority of other eBook retailers, such as Barnes & Noble (Nook), Kobo, and Apple (iBooks).

Even though the eBook format on Amazon is .mobi, they still allow you to upload an .ePub file which they will convert for you. And seeing as every other eBook retailer and distributor on the planet requires an ePub file, there is no reason why you need to export your eBook in any other format. So that's what we're going to do—export your HTML file into an .ePub file which you can upload to all retailers.

First, if you haven't done so already, download Calibre (it's free) here: ***calibre-ebook.com***

EXPORT TO EPUB STEP-BY-STEP:

1. Open Calibre and add the HTML file you created in the last section. You can find the *Add Book* button at the top left of the screen. (Refer to Pic. 11a on page 132 for visual.)

2. Now click *Edit Metadata*, the button to the right of *Add Book*. A dialog box will pop up. Fill in the following details:

Title: *Your Title* (e.g. Star Light)
Title sort: *Your Title* (e.g. Star Light)
Author(s): *Your Name* (e.g. Jessica Bell)
Author sort: *Name, Your* (e.g. Bell, Jessica)
Comments: *your book description*

Also click the *Browse* button and add your front cover. Click *OK*. (Refer to Pic. 11b on page 133 for visual.)

3. Now click on your book in the list so it's highlighted

and then click *Convert books*, the button to the right of *Edit Metadata*. A dialog box will pop up. In the upper right hand corner you need to select the eBook format you want to export in. Make sure you select EPUB, which is the first option in the dropdown menu. (Refer to Pic. 11c on page 134 for visual.)

4. Don't press OK yet. We need to do more here. Click on *Structure Detection* on the left. In this section, you need to leave everything as it is except set *Chapter mark* to *None*. The reason we are setting it to none is because the formatting of the HTML file will already tell Calibre to do what we want. (Refer to Pic. 11d on page 135 for visual.)

5. Now click on *Table of Contents* on the left. What we are going to do here is tell Calibre to use our HTML formatting to create a hyperlinked TOC (contents page) and insert it in the finished product. Ignore everything in this dialog box except:

- Enter in the *Level 1 TOC (XPath expression)* field, the following: *//h:p[re:test(@class, "chap", "i")]*
- Select *Manually fine-tune the TOC after conversion is completed*. (Refer to Pic. 11e on page 136 for visual.)

6. Next up, click on *EPUB Output*. Select the following:

- *Preserve cover aspect ratio*
- *Insert inline Table of Contents*

- *Put inserted Table of Contents at the end of the book.* (Refer to Pic. 11f on page 137 for visual.)
- Click *OK.*

7. You will notice at the bottom right-hand corner that Calibre is generating your ePub. Once the hamster wheel has finished spinning, a dialog box will pop up, which will allow you to look over your Table of Contents.

If everything looks fine, click *OK.* If there is anything you don't want included, such as chapter sub-headings that may have popped up, all you need to do is click on the text you want to remove and then click on *Remove this entry.* Do this for all the entries you don't want visible in your Table of Contents and then click *OK.* (Refer to Pic. 11g on page 138 for visual.)

8. Now you're ready to save your ePub file to your computer. Click on *Save to disk* (located third from the top right), select which folder you want to save it in on your computer and then you're done!

Once it's saved, you will notice there are quite a few different files that have been saved. The only file you will need to upload to retailers/distributors is the ePub file. (Refer to Pic. 11h on page 138 for visual.)

12

UPLOAD YOUR PAPERBACK AND EBOOK TO RETAILERS/DISTRIBUTORS

I don't need to tell you how to do this because each retailer/distributor I've suggested you use is really user-friendly. They give you step by step instructions on how to upload and publish your book, so I would really just be repeating myself here if I outlined the steps for you.

One thing I would like to stress, however, is that you choose the appropriate categories and key words for your book. For two extremely thorough and useful articles about this, and what they mean for you, go to: ***janefriedman.com/2013/07/08/optimizing-metadata*** and ***thebookdesigner.com/2014/09/7-tips-***

for-metadata-magic-for-self-publishers

I would also like to advise you to preview what your book will look like on a Kindle and an ePub Reader.

To preview what it looks like on an ePub reader, you can download Adobe Digital Editions (for free): ***adobe.com/solutions/ebook/digital-editions/download.html***

You can preview it on Kindle once you've uploaded it to Kindle Direct Publishing as they have an inbuilt previewer you can use before you hit that publish button.

Can you believe you're almost done?

Do you realize you're going to have a published book within the next 24 hours?

Congratulations!!!

13

NEED EXTRA SELF-PUBLISHING ADVICE?

Book yourself in for a 45-minute one-on-one casual consultation via Skype (with video on or off, your choice). I'm happy to talk about all things writing, editing and self-publishing. Sessions cost 25 Euros and can be paid via PayPal. If you require more time, that can be arranged and a price privately negotiated.

Email me to inquire about availability and book yourself in: ***jessica.carmen.bell@gmail.com***

14

RECOMMENDED NEXT STEPS

Visit my website for lots of other goodies for writers: ***jessicabellauthor.com***

Join the Alliance of Independent Authors for education, advocacy, help, great discounts on services, and networking with other self-published authors: ***allianceindependentauthors.org***. As a member, you get great discounts with IngramSpark. You also get 50% off a professional book cover design from me.

Start a website/blog, join Twitter and Facebook and start networking with potential readers. You can get some great advice here: ***thecreativepenn.com/marketing***

Consider releasing your title as an audio book: ***acx.com***

Write and publish another book! The best way to gain traction in this industry is to have a backlist of books.

Start building it. Now.

ACKNOWLEDGEMENTS

Many thanks to the authors who were my "guinea pigs" and offered invaluable feedback on an early draft of this book: Glynis Smy, Terry Freedman, and Misha Gericke. Also great thanks to Kevin Booth who copyedited my final manuscript on such short notice. I wouldn't be where I am today if it weren't for Dawn Ius, who is my biggest, most reliable, and most generous go-to person for emotional and creative support and encouragement. I couldn't do this without you, Dawn. Of course, how could I forget my partner, Spilios Tzemos, for putting up with my ridiculous hours sitting at my computer. Being with you is like the world has been cleansed of all hate. And last but not least, my parents, Erika Bach and Demetri Vlass for always believing in me. I love you both, dearly.

If you found this book helpful, it would be extremely appreciated if you could post a review at the retailer you purchased it from.

Interested in my upcoming titles?
You can sign up for my newsletter at ***jessicabellauthor.com*** *to stay up-to-date.*

PICTURE AIDS

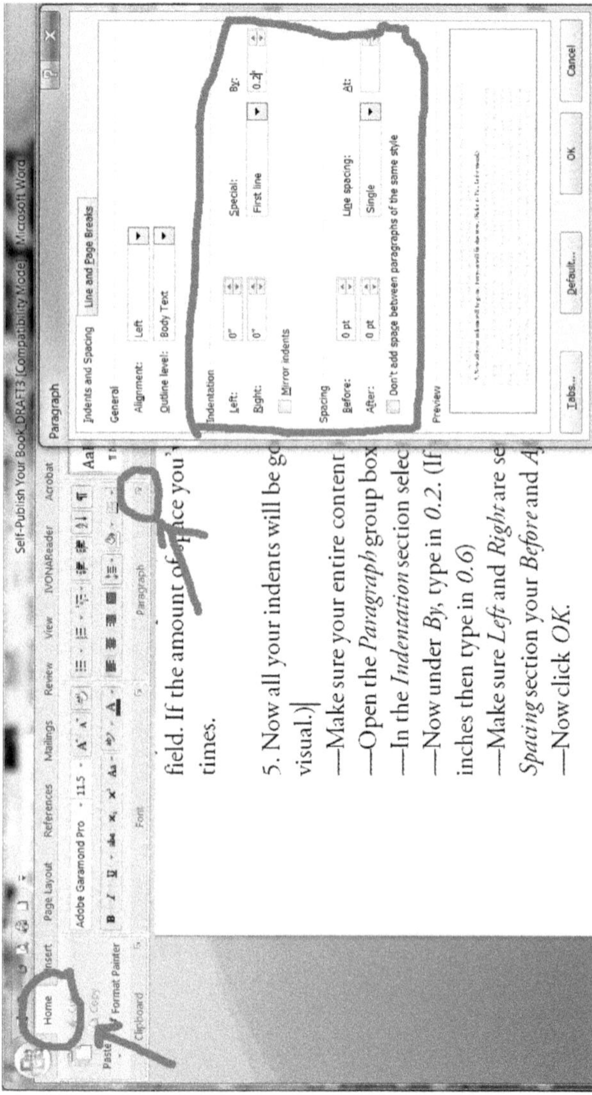
Self-Publish Your Book_DRAFT3 [Compatibility Mode] - Microsoft Word
Home
Insert
Page Layout
References
Mailings
Review
View
IVONAReader
Acrobat
Paste
Copy
Format Painter
Clipboard
Adobe Garamond Pro
11.5
Font
Paragraph
Indents and Spacing
Line and Page Breaks
General
Alignment:
Left
Outline level:
Body Text
Indentation
Left:
0"
Right:
0"
Special:
First line
By:
0.2"
Mirror indents
Spacing
Before:
0 pt
After:
0 pt
Line spacing:
Single
At:
Don't add space between paragraphs of the same style
Preview
Tabs...
Default...
OK
Cancel
field. If the amount of space you
times.
5. Now all your indents will be go
visual.)
—Make sure your entire content
—Open the Paragraph group box
—In the Indentation section selec
—Now under By, type in 0.2. (If
inches then type in 0.6)
—Make sure Left and Right are se
Spacing section your Before and A
—Now click OK.

Pic. 1a

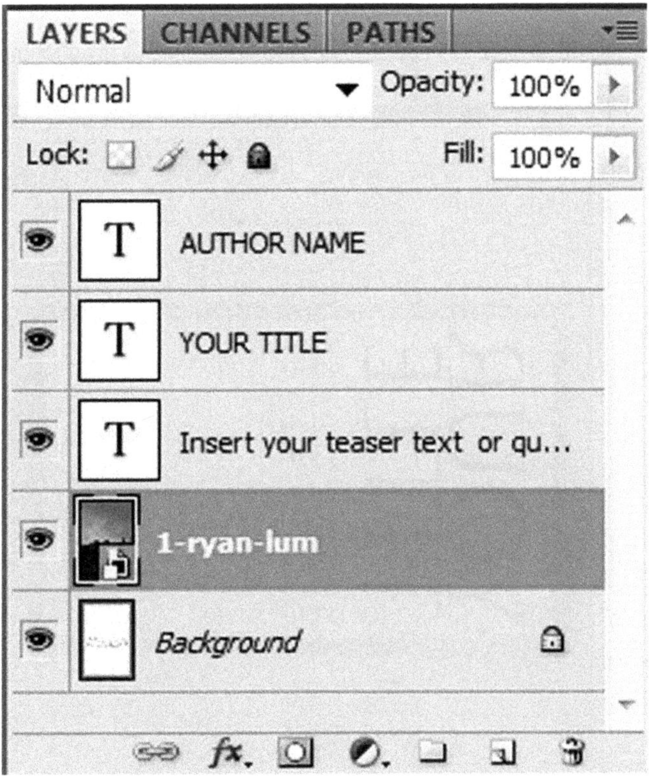
LAYERS
CHANNELS
PATHS
Normal
Opacity: 100%
Lock:
Fill: 100%
AUTHOR NAME
YOUR TITLE
Insert your teaser text or qu...
1-ryan-lum
Background

Pic. 2a

YOUR TITLE
The red area is the bleed area. Though you do not need a bleed area for an eBook, you are going to use this to create your paperback cover, which will have a bleed area. So you need to make sure that whatever is in the red section, you do not need to be visible, as much of it will get trimmed off. That said, you still must cover it with your image, otherwise you may end up with red edges!
AUTHOR NAME

Pic. 2b

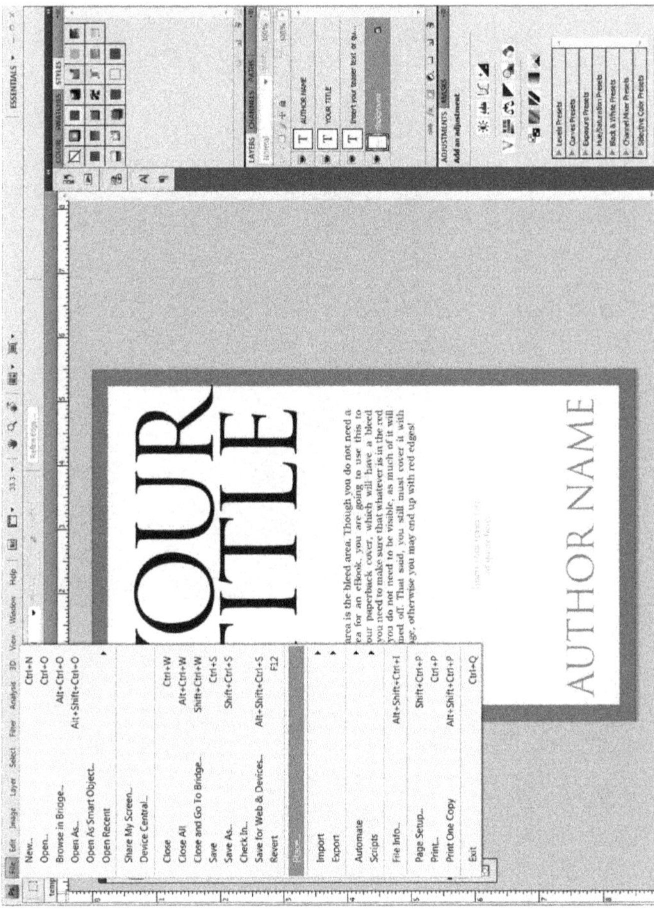

Pic. 2c

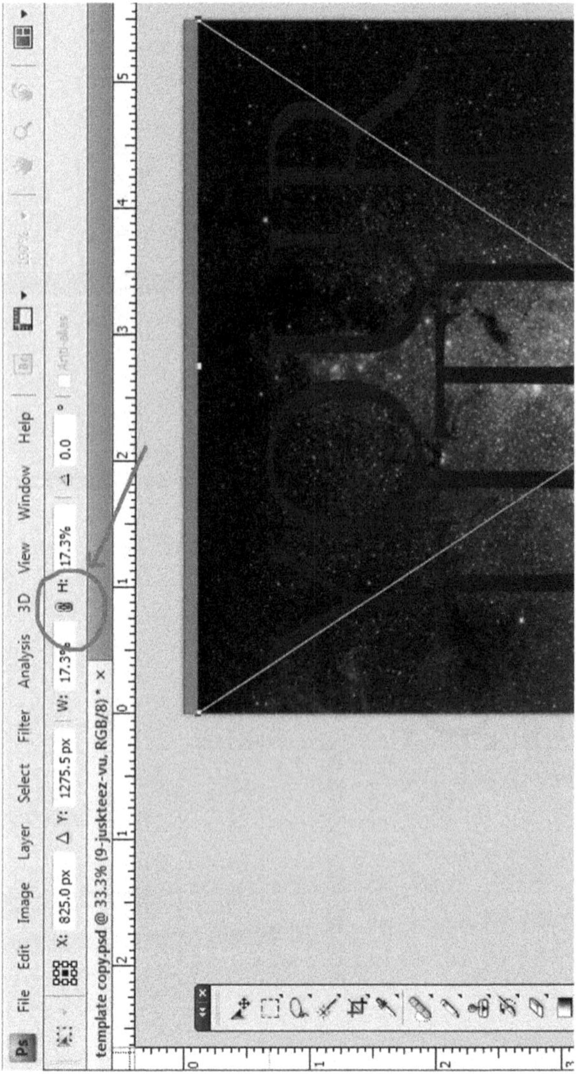
File Edit Image Layer Select Filter Analysis 3D View Window Help
X: 825.0 px
Y: 1275.5 px
W: 17.3%
H: 17.3%
0.0
template copy.psd @ 33.3% (9-juskteez-vu, RGB/8) *

Pic. 2d

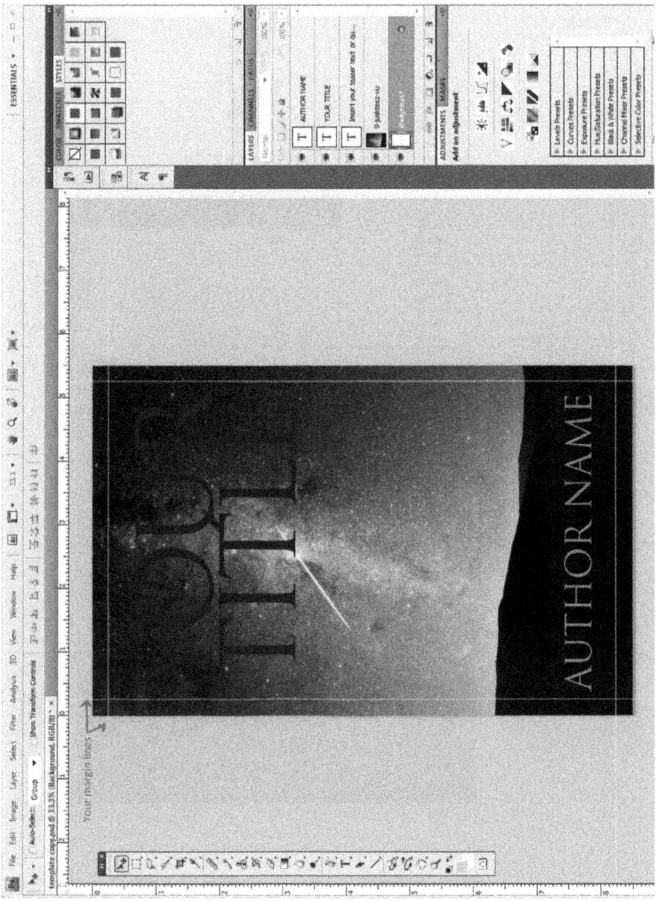

Pic. 2e

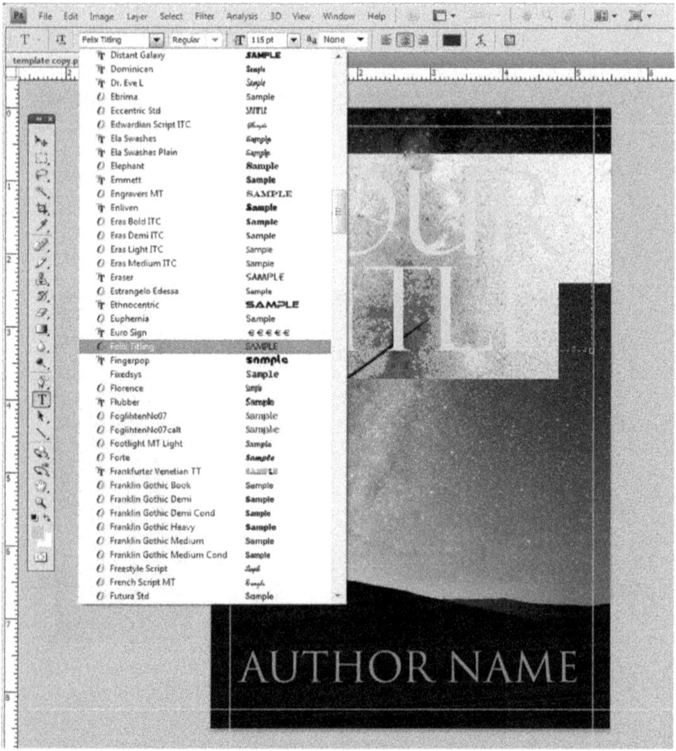

Pic. 2f

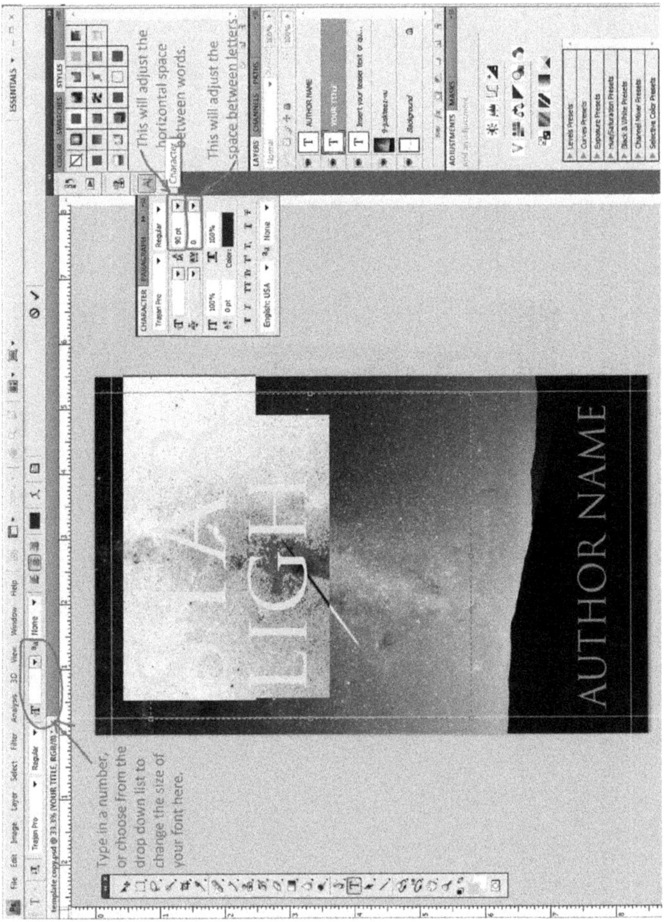
Type in a number, or choose from the drop down list to change the size of your font here.
This will adjust the horizontal space between words.
This will adjust the space between letters.
AUTHOR NAME

Pic. 2g

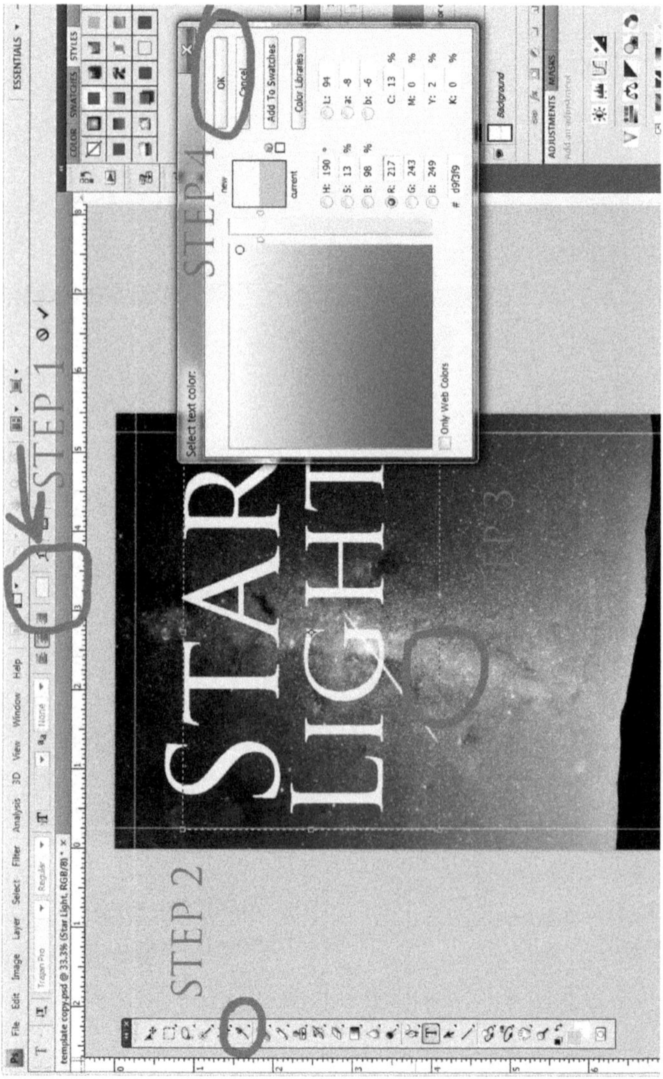
STEP 1
STEP 2
STEP 4
STAR
LIGHT
Select text color:
OK
Cancel
Add To Swatches
Color Libraries
Only Web Colors

Pic. 2h

STAR
LIGHT
One blackout.
One star.
A million heroes.
JESSICA BELL

Pic. 2i

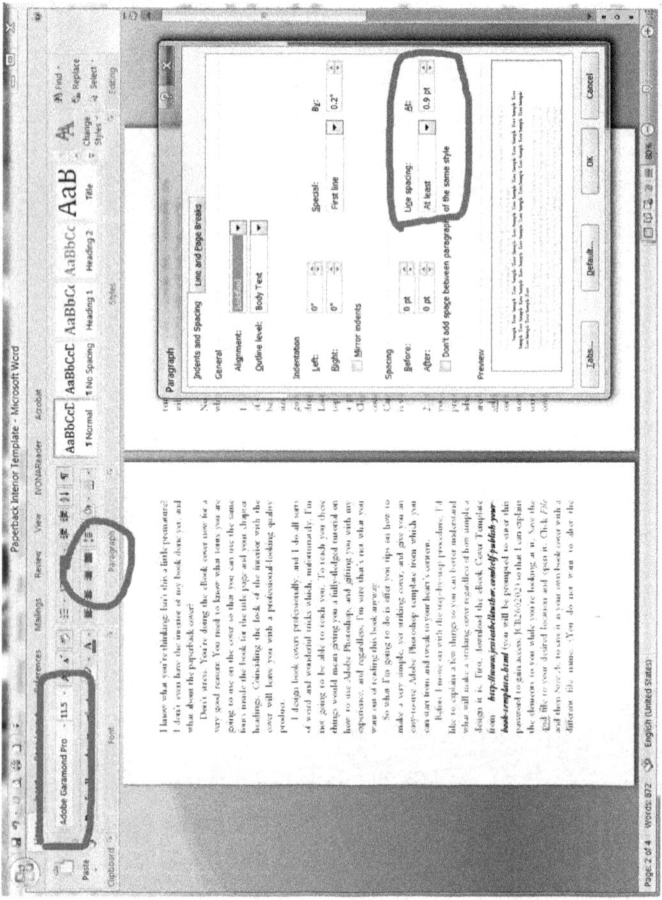

Pic. 4a

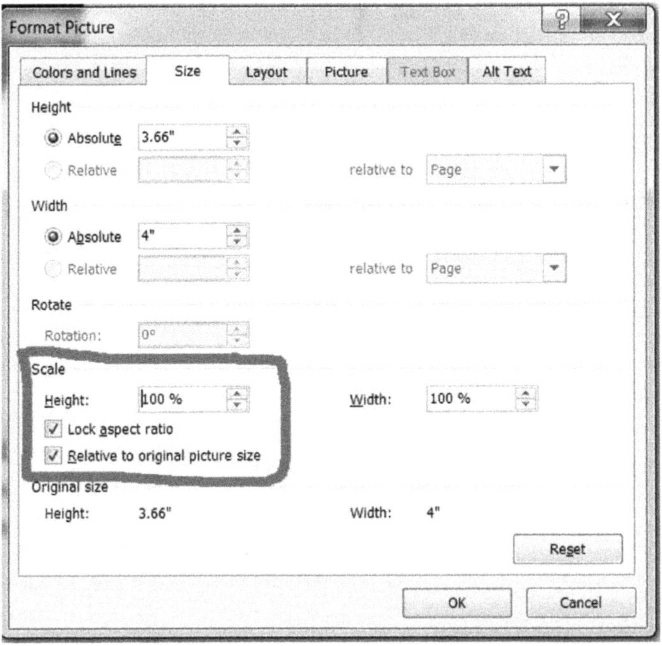
Format Picture
Colors and Lines
Size
Layout
Picture
Text Box
Alt Text
Height
Absolute
3.66"
Relative
relative to
Page
Width
Absolute
4"
Relative
relative to
Page
Rotate
Rotation:
0°
Scale
Height:
100 %
Width:
100 %
Lock aspect ratio
Relative to original picture size
Original size
Height:
3.66"
Width:
4"
Reset
OK
Cancel

Pic. 4b

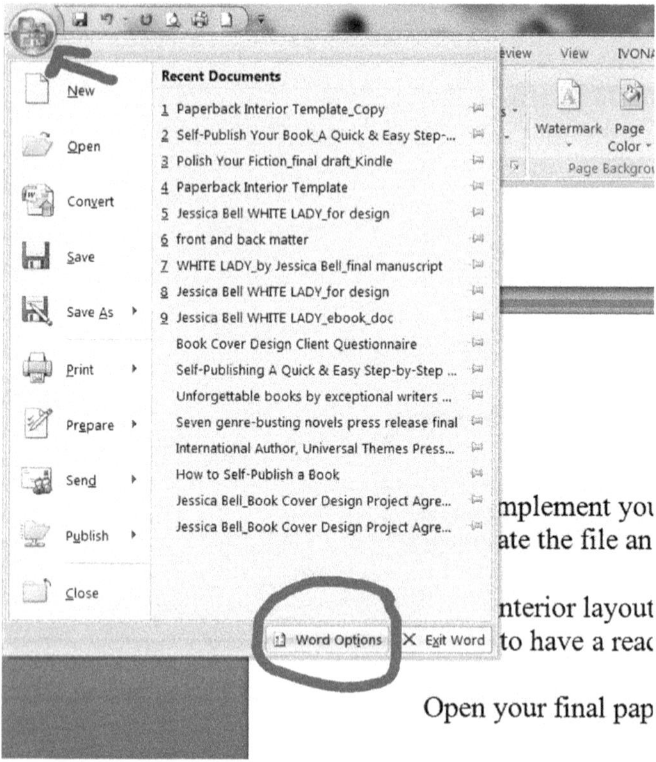
Recent Documents
New
Open
Convert
Save
Save As
Print
Prepare
Send
Publish
Close
1 Paperback Interior Template_Copy
2 Self-Publish Your Book_A Quick & Easy Step-...
3 Polish Your Fiction_final draft_Kindle
4 Paperback Interior Template
5 Jessica Bell WHITE LADY_for design
6 front and back matter
7 WHITE LADY_by Jessica Bell_final manuscript
8 Jessica Bell WHITE LADY_for design
9 Jessica Bell WHITE LADY_ebook_doc
Book Cover Design Client Questionnaire
Self-Publishing A Quick & Easy Step-by-Step ...
Unforgettable books by exceptional writers ...
Seven genre-busting novels press release final
International Author, Universal Themes Press...
How to Self-Publish a Book
Jessica Bell_Book Cover Design Project Agre...
Jessica Bell_Book Cover Design Project Agre...
View
Watermark
Page Color
Word Options
Exit Word
Open your final pap

Pic. 5a

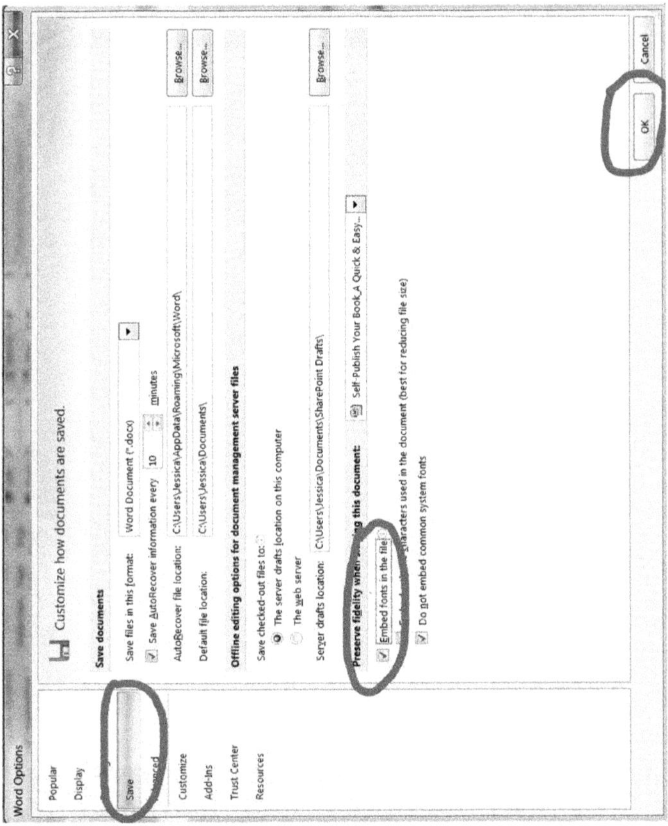
Word Options
Popular
Display
Save
Customize
Add-Ins
Trust Center
Resources
Customize how documents are saved.
Save documents
Save files in this format:
Word Document (*.docx)
Save AutoRecover information every
10
minutes
AutoRecover file location:
C:\Users\Jessica\AppData\Roaming\Microsoft\Word\
Browse...
Default file location:
C:\Users\Jessica\Documents\
Browse...
Offline editing options for document management server files
Save checked-out files to:
The server drafts location on this computer
The web server
Server drafts location:
C:\Users\Jessica\Documents\SharePoint Drafts\
Browse...
Self-Publish Your Book_A Quick & Easy...
Embed fonts in the file
characters used in the document (best for reducing file size)
Do not embed common system fonts
OK
Cancel

Pic. 5b

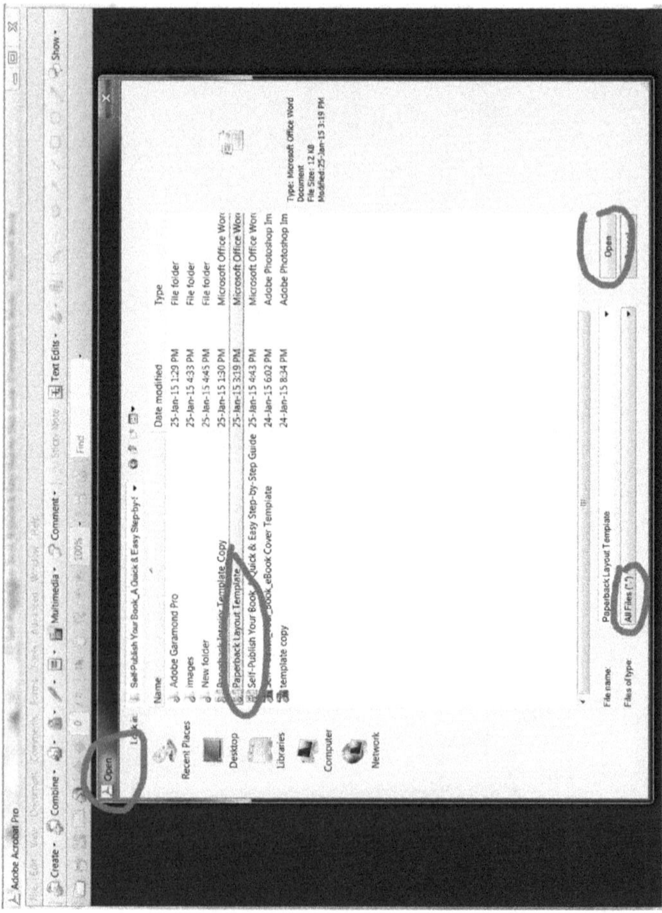
Adobe Acrobat Pro
Create
Combine
Multimedia
Comment
Text Edits
Show
Open
Name
Date modified
Type
Adobe Garamond Pro
images
New folder
Paperback Layout Template
Self-Publish Your Book
template copy
Recent Places
Desktop
Libraries
Computer
Network
File name:
Paperback Layout Template
Files of type:
All Files (*.*)
Open

Pic. 6a

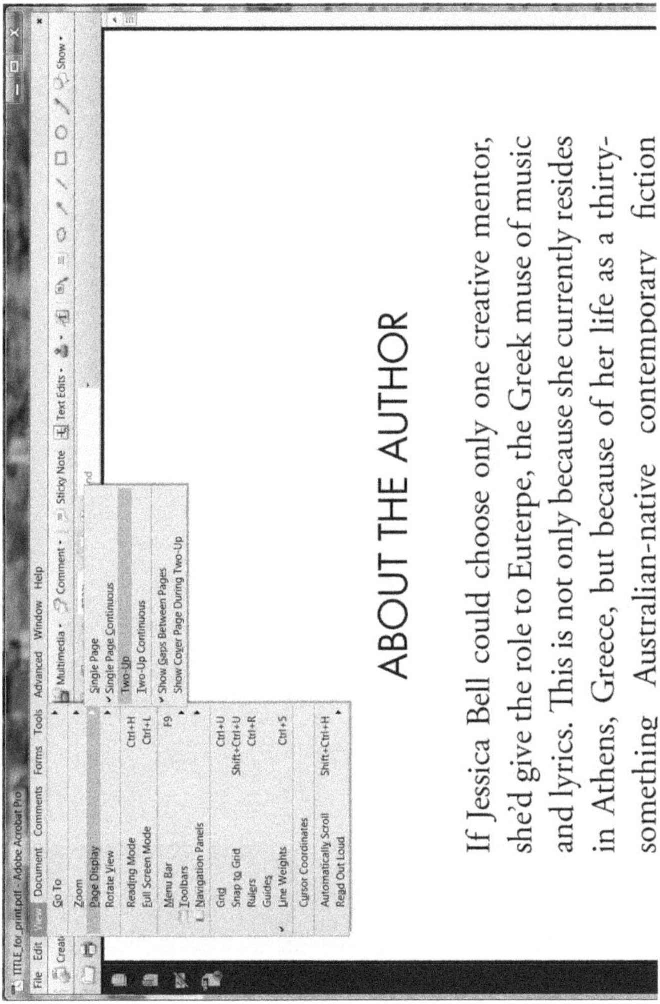
TITLE_for_print.pdf - Adobe Acrobat Pro
File Edit View Document Comments Forms Tools Advanced Window Help
Go To
Zoom
Page Display
Rotate View
Reading Mode Ctrl+H
Full Screen Mode Ctrl+L
Menu Bar F9
Toolbars
Navigation Panels
Grid Ctrl+U
Snap to Grid Shift+Ctrl+U
Rulers Ctrl+R
Guides
Line Weights Ctrl+5
Cursor Coordinates
Automatically Scroll Shift+Ctrl+H
Read Out Loud
Single Page
Single Page Continuous
Two-Up
Two-Up Continuous
Show Gaps Between Pages
Show Cover Page During Two-Up
Multimedia Comment Sticky Note Text Edits Show
ABOUT THE AUTHOR
If Jessica Bell could choose only one creative mentor, she'd give the role to Euterpe, the Greek muse of music and lyrics. This is not only because she currently resides in Athens, Greece, but because of her life as a thirty-something Australian-native contemporary fiction

Pic. 6b

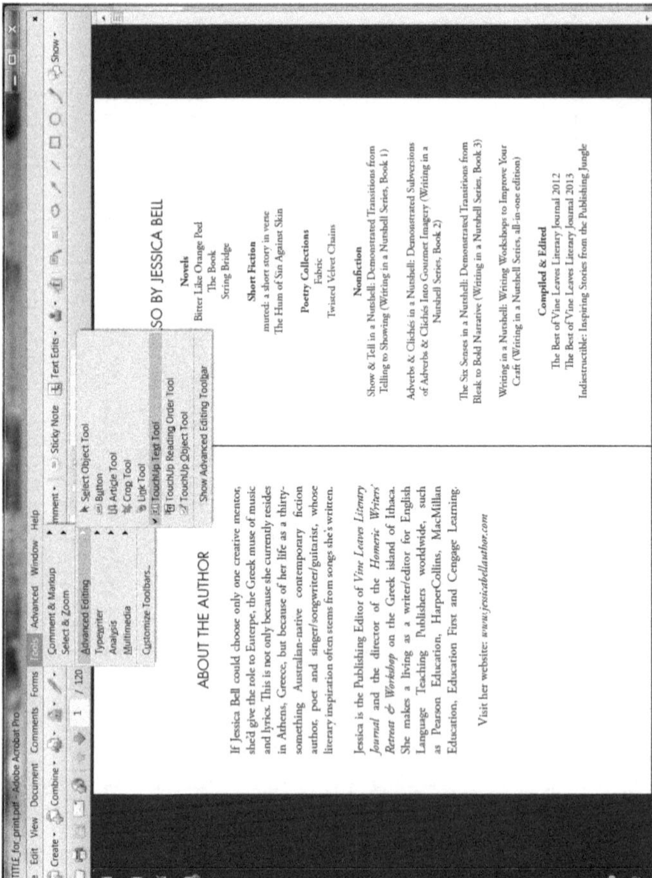
TITLE_for_print.pdf - Adobe Acrobat Pro
File Edit View Document Comments Forms Tools Advanced Window Help
Comment & Markup
Select & Zoom
Advanced Editing
Typewriter
Analysis
Multimedia
Customize Toolbars...
Select Object Tool
Button
Article Tool
Crop Tool
Link Tool
TouchUp Text Tool
TouchUp Reading Order Tool
TouchUp Object Tool
Show Advanced Editing Toolbar
Sticky Note
Text Edits
Show
ABOUT THE AUTHOR
If Jessica Bell could choose only one creative mentor, she'd give the role to Euterpe, the Greek muse of music and lyrics. This is not only because she currently resides in Athens, Greece, but because of her life as a thirty-something Australian-native contemporary fiction author, poet and singer/songwriter/guitarist, whose literary inspiration often stems from songs she's written.
Jessica is the Publishing Editor of Vine Leaves Literary Journal and the director of the Homeric Writers' Retreat & Workshop on the Greek island of Ithaca. She makes a living as a writer/editor for English Language Teaching Publishers worldwide, such as Pearson Education, HarperCollins, MacMillan Education, Education First and Cengage Learning.
Visit her website: www.jessicabellauthor.com
SO BY JESSICA BELL
Novels
Bitter Like Orange Peel
The Book
String Bridge
Short Fiction
muted: a short story in verse
The Hum of Sin Against Skin
Poetry Collections
Fabric
Twisted Velvet Chains
Nonfiction
Show & Tell in a Nutshell: Demonstrated Transitions from Telling to Showing (Writing in a Nutshell Series, Book 1)
Adverbs & Clichés in a Nutshell: Demonstrated Subversions of Adverbs & Clichés Into Gourmet Imagery (Writing in a Nutshell Series, Book 2)
The Six Senses in a Nutshell: Demonstrated Transitions from Bleak to Bold Narrative (Writing in a Nutshell Series, Book 3)
Writing in a Nutshell: Writing Workshops to Improve Your Craft (Writing in a Nutshell Series, all-in-one edition)
Compiled & Edited
The Best of Vine Leaves Literary Journal 2012
The Best of Vine Leaves Literary Journal 2013
Indiestructible: Inspiring Stories from the Publishing Jungle

Pic. 6c

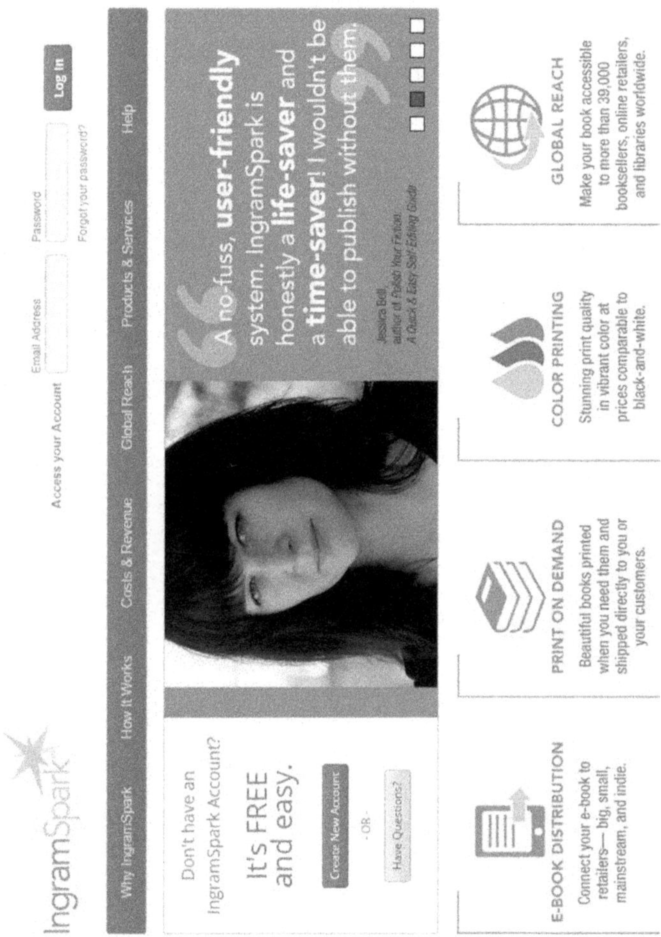
IngramSpark
Access your Account
Email Address
Password
Forgot your password?
Log In
Why IngramSpark
How It Works
Costs & Revenue
Global Reach
Products & Services
Help
Don't have an IngramSpark Account?
It's FREE and easy.
Create New Account
- OR -
Have Questions?
A no-fuss, user-friendly system. IngramSpark is honestly a life-saver and a time-saver! I wouldn't be able to publish without them.
Jessica Bell, author of Polish Your Fiction: A Quick & Easy Self-Editing Guide
E-BOOK DISTRIBUTION
Connect your e-book to retailers— big, small, mainstream, and indie.
PRINT ON DEMAND
Beautiful books printed when you need them and shipped directly to you or your customers.
COLOR PRINTING
Stunning print quality in vibrant color at prices comparable to black-and-white.
GLOBAL REACH
Make your book accessible to more than 39,000 booksellers, online retailers, and libraries worldwide.

Pic. 7a

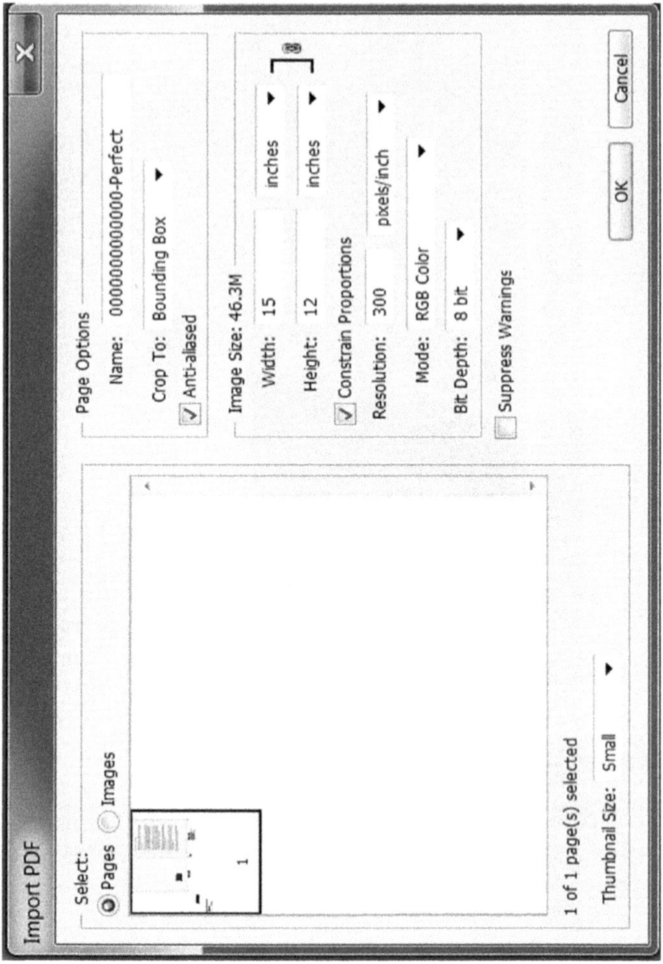
Import PDF
Select:
Pages
Images
1
1 of 1 page(s) selected
Thumbnail Size: Small
Page Options
Name: 0000000000000-Perfect
Crop To: Bounding Box
Anti-aliased
Image Size: 46.3M
Width: 15 inches
Height: 12 inches
Constrain Proportions
Resolution: 300 pixels/inch
Mode: RGB Color
Bit Depth: 8 bit
Suppress Warnings
OK
Cancel

Pic. 9a

Template Instructions:
• Pink (Safe) Area: All text, important images, logos and barcode should remain inside the pink areas.
• Blue (Bleed) Area: All backgrounds should extend throughout the blue and pink areas. If a white background is desired, create a white box that covers the entire bleed area.
• White (Template) Area: No artwork should extend into the white areas that contain the black trim and fold marks and template info. Please leave all elements outside of the pink and blue areas unaltered.
• Barcode Placement: The provided barcode may be moved to any location within the pink area of the back cover.
• Document Size: The overall document size for this template is shown in the lower left corner. The final cover PDF submitted must match this size.
Pink and blue boxes must be completely covered when cover is submitted.

Pic. 9b

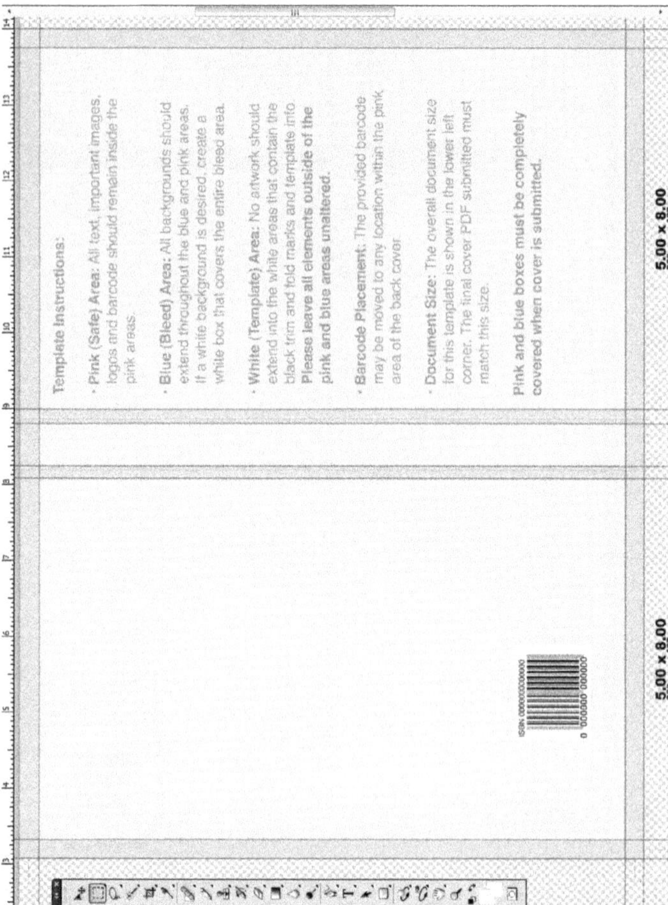
Template Instructions:
· Pink (Safe) Area: All text, important images, logos and barcode should remain inside the pink areas.
· Blue (Bleed) Area: All backgrounds should extend throughout the blue and pink areas. If a white background is desired, create a white box that covers the entire bleed area.
· White (Template) Area: No artwork should extend into the white areas that contain the black trim and fold marks and template info. Please leave all elements outside of the pink and blue areas unaltered.
· Barcode Placement: The provided barcode may be moved to any location within the pink area of the back cover.
· Document Size: The overall document size for this template is shown in the lower left corner. The final cover PDF submitted must match this size.
Pink and blue boxes must be completely covered when cover is submitted.
5.00 x 8.00
5.00 x 8.00

Pic. 9c

STAR
LIGHT
One black out.
One star.
A million heroes.
JESSICA BELL
5.00 x 8.00
5.00 x 8.00

Pic. 9d

STAR
LIGHT
One black out.
One star.
A million heroes.
JESSICA BELL
5.00 x 8.00
5.00 x 8.00

Pic. 9e

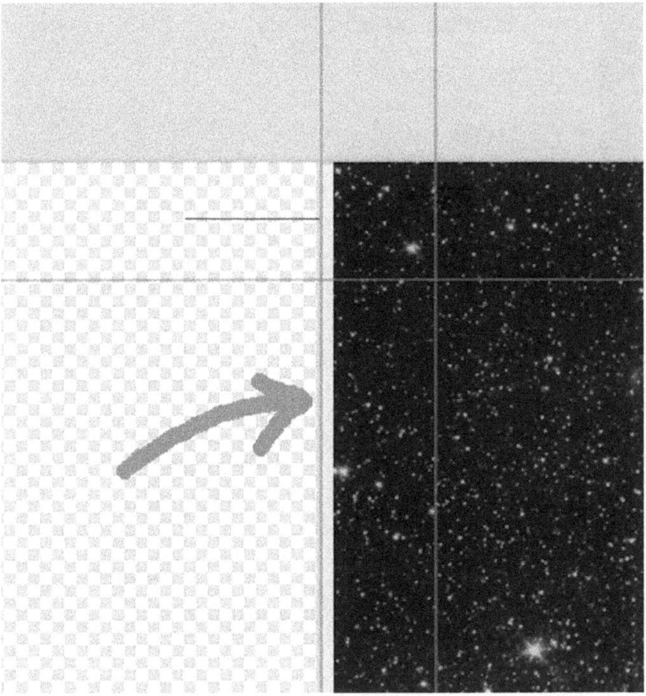

Pic. 9f

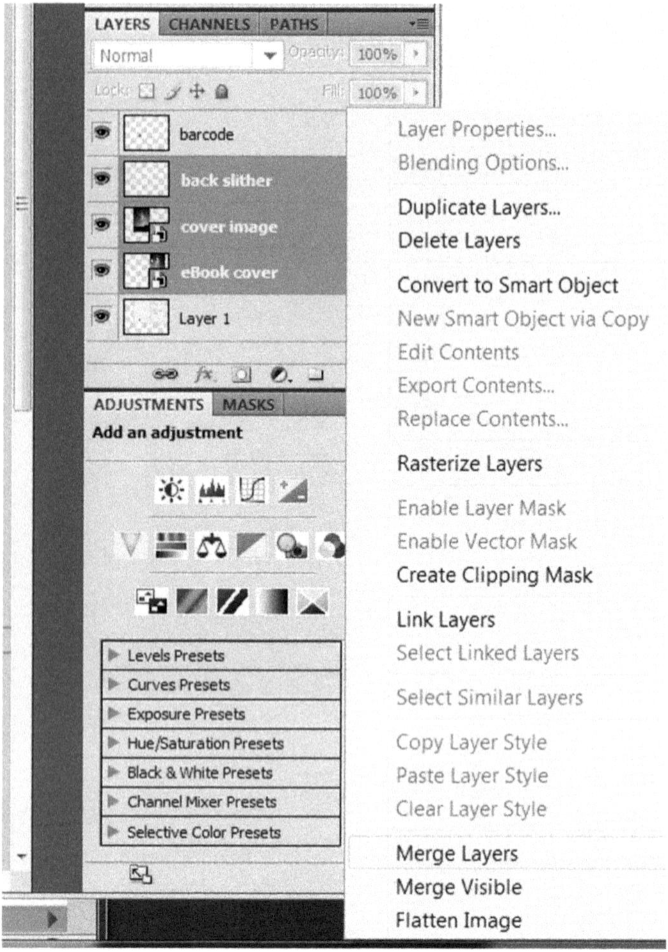
LAYERS
CHANNELS
PATHS
Normal
Opacity:
100%
Lock:
Fill:
100%
barcode
back slither
cover image
eBook cover
Layer 1
ADJUSTMENTS
MASKS
Add an adjustment
Levels Presets
Curves Presets
Exposure Presets
Hue/Saturation Presets
Black & White Presets
Channel Mixer Presets
Selective Color Presets
Layer Properties...
Blending Options...
Duplicate Layers...
Delete Layers
Convert to Smart Object
New Smart Object via Copy
Edit Contents
Export Contents...
Replace Contents...
Rasterize Layers
Enable Layer Mask
Enable Vector Mask
Create Clipping Mask
Link Layers
Select Linked Layers
Select Similar Layers
Copy Layer Style
Paste Layer Style
Clear Layer Style
Merge Layers
Merge Visible
Flatten Image

Pic. 9g

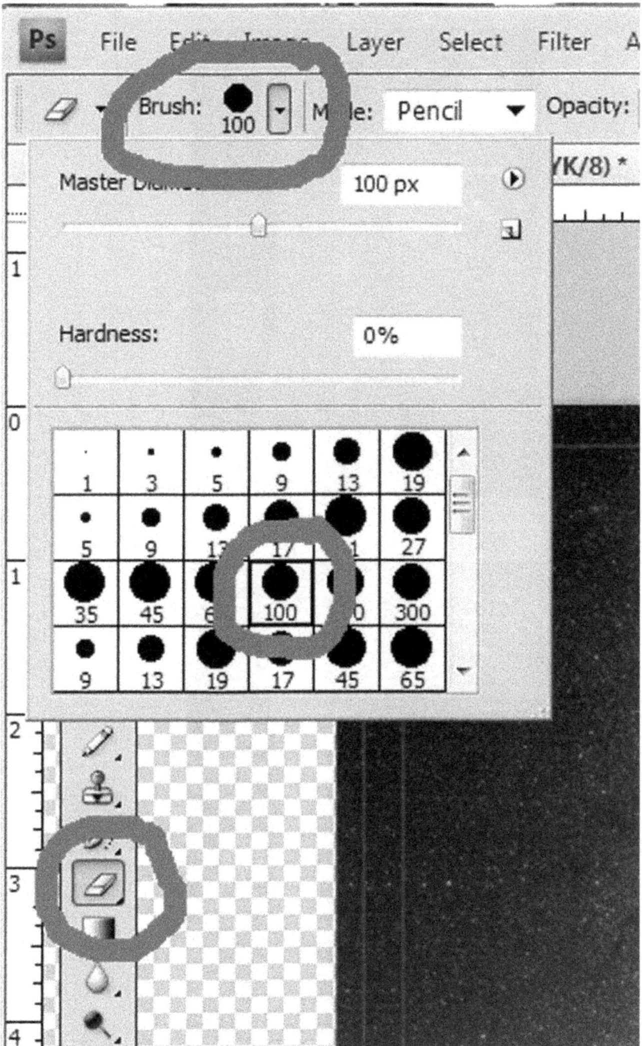
Ps
File
Layer
Select
Filter
Brush:
100
Pencil
Opacity:
100 px
Hardness:
0%
1
3
5
9
13
19
27
35
45
100
300
17
65

Pic. 9h

STAR
LIGHT
One black out.
One star.
A million heroes.
JESSICA BELL
AFTER
STAR
LIGHT
One black out.
One star.
A million heroes.
JESSICA BELL
BEFORE

Pic. 9i

Justify last left
One black out.
One star.
A million heroes.
JESSICA BELL

Pic. 9j

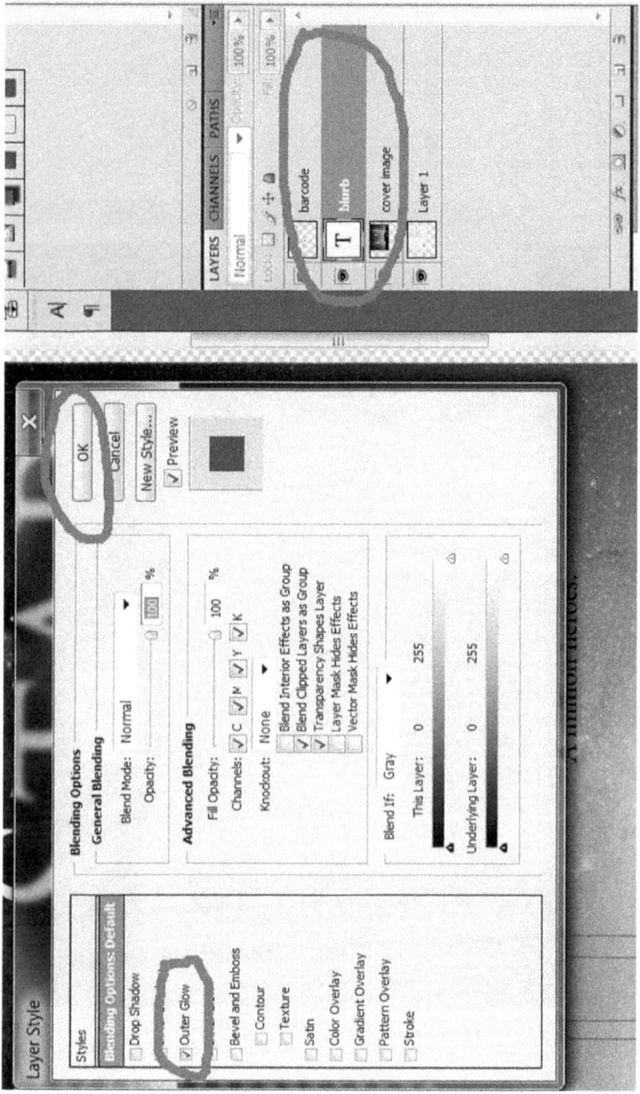
Layer Style
Styles
Blending Options: Default
Drop Shadow
Outer Glow
Bevel and Emboss
Contour
Texture
Satin
Color Overlay
Gradient Overlay
Pattern Overlay
Stroke
Blending Options
General Blending
Blend Mode: Normal
Opacity: 100 %
Advanced Blending
Fill Opacity: 100 %
Channels: C M Y K
Knockout: None
Blend Interior Effects as Group
Blend Clipped Layers as Group
Transparency Shapes Layer
Layer Mask Hides Effects
Vector Mask Hides Effects
Blend If: Gray
This Layer: 0 255
Underlying Layer: 0 255
OK
Cancel
New Style...
Preview
LAYERS CHANNELS PATHS
Normal
barcode
blurb
cover image
Layer 1

Pic. 9k

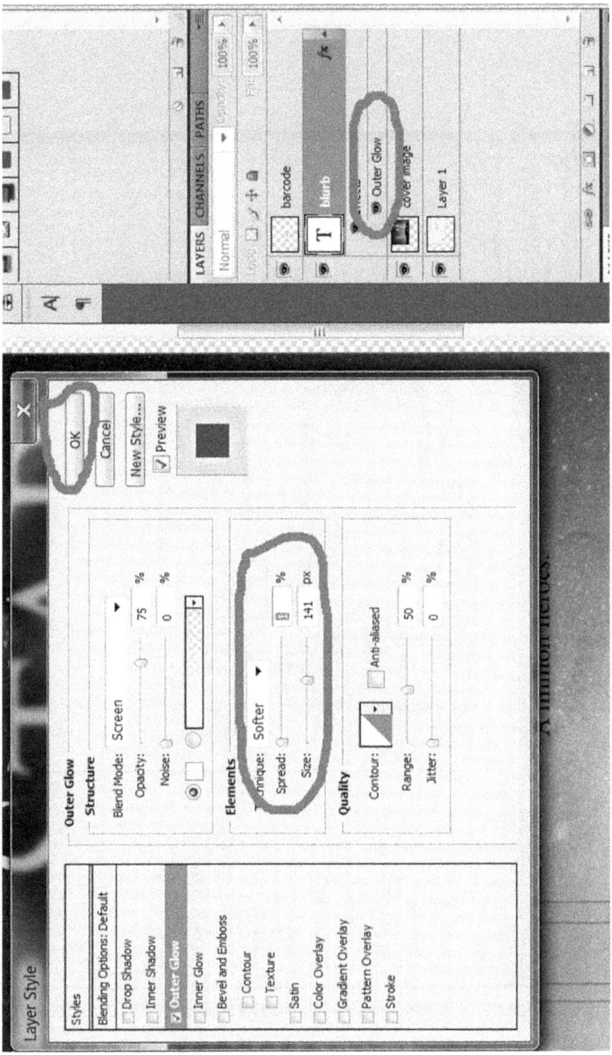
Layer Style
Styles
Blending Options: Default
Drop Shadow
Inner Shadow
Outer Glow
Inner Glow
Bevel and Emboss
Contour
Texture
Satin
Color Overlay
Gradient Overlay
Pattern Overlay
Stroke
Outer Glow
Structure
Blend Mode: Screen
Opacity: 75 %
Noise: 0 %
Elements
Softer
Spread: %
Size: 141 px
Quality
Contour:
Anti-aliased
Range: 50 %
Jitter: 0 %
OK
Cancel
New Style...
Preview
LAYERS
CHANNELS
PATHS
Normal
Opacity: 100%
Fill: 100%
barcode
blurb
Outer Glow
cover image
Layer 1

Pic. 9l

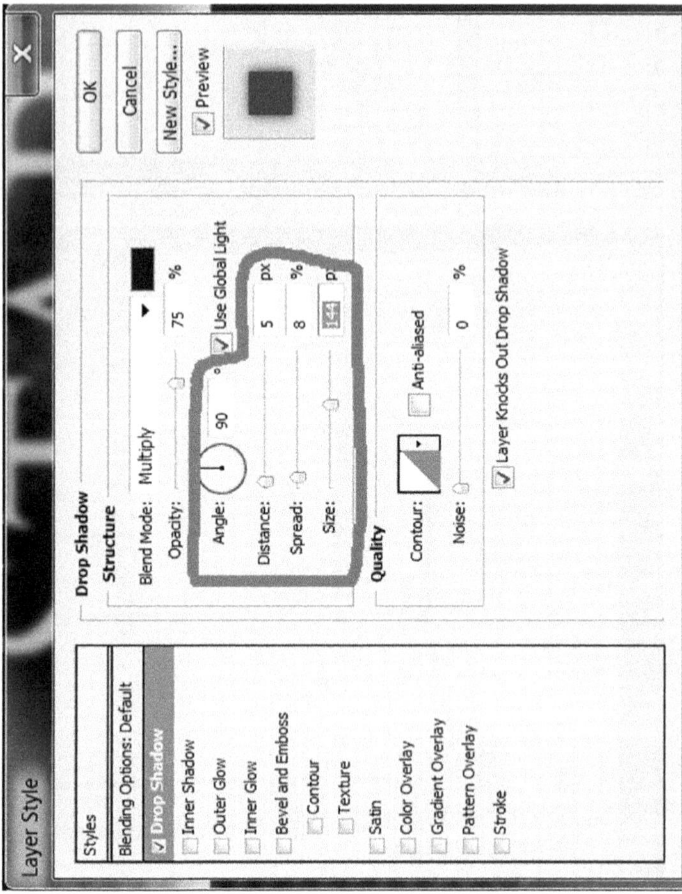
Layer Style
OK
Cancel
New Style...
Preview
Styles
Blending Options: Default
Drop Shadow
Inner Shadow
Outer Glow
Inner Glow
Bevel and Emboss
Contour
Texture
Satin
Color Overlay
Gradient Overlay
Pattern Overlay
Stroke
Drop Shadow
Structure
Blend Mode: Multiply
Opacity: 75 %
Angle: 90 °
Use Global Light
Distance: 5 px
Spread: 8 %
Size:
Quality
Contour:
Anti-aliased
Noise: 0 %
Layer Knocks Out Drop Shadow

Pic. 9m

ISBN 978-0-9925097-3-6
90000
9 780992 509736
Cover & Interior design: Jessica Bell
Cover Images: © Shutterstock.com
Vine Leaves Press
Melbourne, Vic, Australia

Pic. 9n

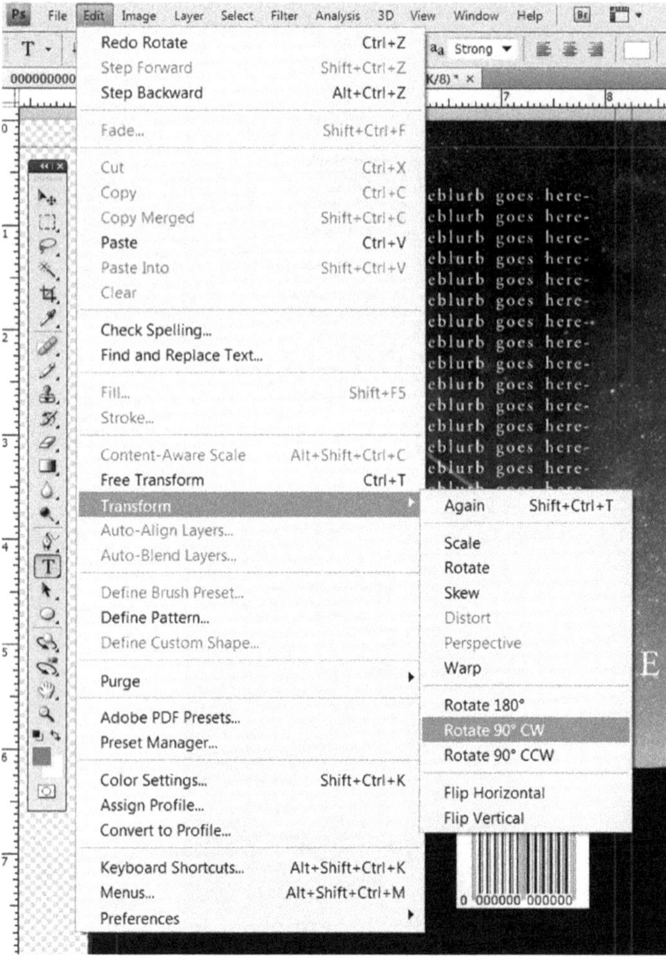
File
Edit
Image
Layer
Select
Filter
Analysis
3D
View
Window
Help
Strong
Redo Rotate Ctrl+Z
Step Forward Shift+Ctrl+Z
Step Backward Alt+Ctrl+Z
Fade... Shift+Ctrl+F
Cut Ctrl+X
Copy Ctrl+C
Copy Merged Shift+Ctrl+C
Paste Ctrl+V
Paste Into Shift+Ctrl+V
Clear
Check Spelling...
Find and Replace Text...
Fill... Shift+F5
Stroke...
Content-Aware Scale Alt+Shift+Ctrl+C
Free Transform Ctrl+T
Transform
Auto-Align Layers...
Auto-Blend Layers...
Define Brush Preset...
Define Pattern...
Define Custom Shape...
Purge
Adobe PDF Presets...
Preset Manager...
Color Settings... Shift+Ctrl+K
Assign Profile...
Convert to Profile...
Keyboard Shortcuts... Alt+Shift+Ctrl+K
Menus... Alt+Shift+Ctrl+M
Preferences
Again Shift+Ctrl+T
Scale
Rotate
Skew
Distort
Perspective
Warp
Rotate 180°
Rotate 90° CW
Rotate 90° CCW
Flip Horizontal
Flip Vertical

Pic. 9o

STAR
LIGHT
One black out.
One star.
A million heroes.
JESSICA BELL
STAR LIGHT
JESSICA BELL
Other information
Other information
Other information

Pic. 9p

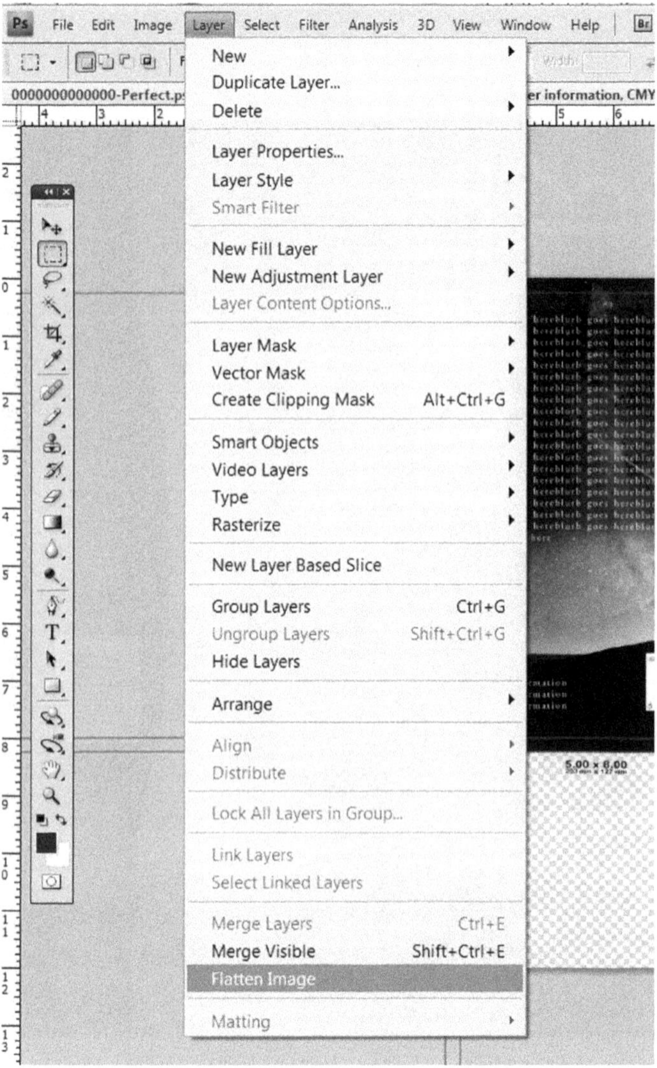
Ps
File
Edit
Image
Layer
Select
Filter
Analysis
3D
View
Window
Help
0000000000000-Perfect.ps
er information, CMY
New
Duplicate Layer...
Delete
Layer Properties...
Layer Style
Smart Filter
New Fill Layer
New Adjustment Layer
Layer Content Options...
Layer Mask
Vector Mask
Create Clipping Mask Alt+Ctrl+G
Smart Objects
Video Layers
Type
Rasterize
New Layer Based Slice
Group Layers Ctrl+G
Ungroup Layers Shift+Ctrl+G
Hide Layers
Arrange
Align
Distribute
Lock All Layers in Group...
Link Layers
Select Linked Layers
Merge Layers Ctrl+E
Merge Visible Shift+Ctrl+E
Flatten Image
Matting
5.00 x 8.00

Pic. 9q

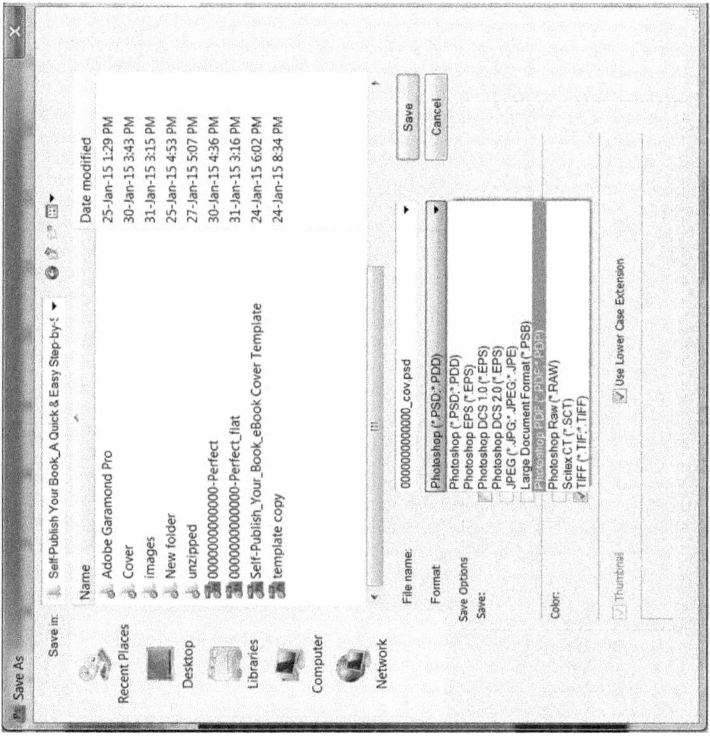

Pic. 9r

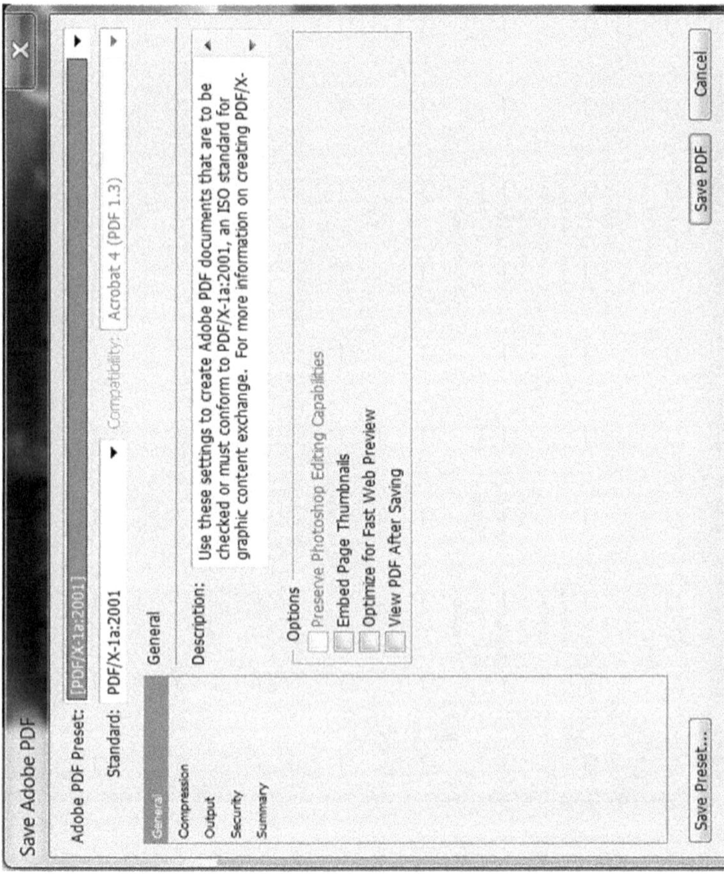
Save Adobe PDF
Adobe PDF Preset: [PDF/X-1a:2001]
Standard: PDF/X-1a:2001
Compatibility: Acrobat 4 (PDF 1.3)
General
Compression
Output
Security
Summary
General
Description:
Use these settings to create Adobe PDF documents that are to be checked or must conform to PDF/X-1a:2001, an ISO standard for graphic content exchange. For more information on creating PDF/X-
Options
Preserve Photoshop Editing Capabilities
Embed Page Thumbnails
Optimize for Fast Web Preview
View PDF After Saving
Save Preset...
Save PDF
Cancel

Pic. 9s

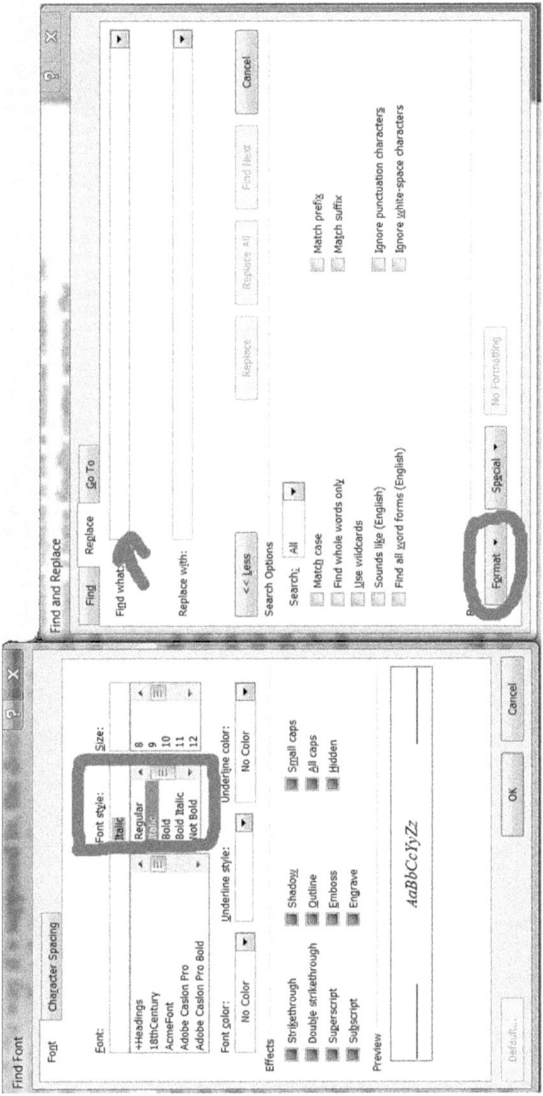
Find and Replace
Find
Replace
Go To
Find what:
Replace with:
<< Less
Replace
Replace All
Find Next
Cancel
Search Options
Search:
All
Match case
Find whole words only
Use wildcards
Sounds like (English)
Find all word forms (English)
Match prefix
Match suffix
Ignore punctuation characters
Ignore white-space characters
Format
Special
No Formatting
Find Font
Font
Character Spacing
Font:
Font style:
Size:
+Headings
18thCentury
AcmeFont
Adobe Caslon Pro
Adobe Caslon Pro Bold
Italic
Regular
Bold
Bold Italic
Not Bold
8
9
10
11
12
Font color:
No Color
Underline style:
Underline color:
Effects
Strikethrough
Double strikethrough
Superscript
Subscript
Shadow
Outline
Emboss
Engrave
Small caps
All caps
Hidden
Preview
AaBbCcYyZz
Default...
OK
Cancel

Pic. 10a

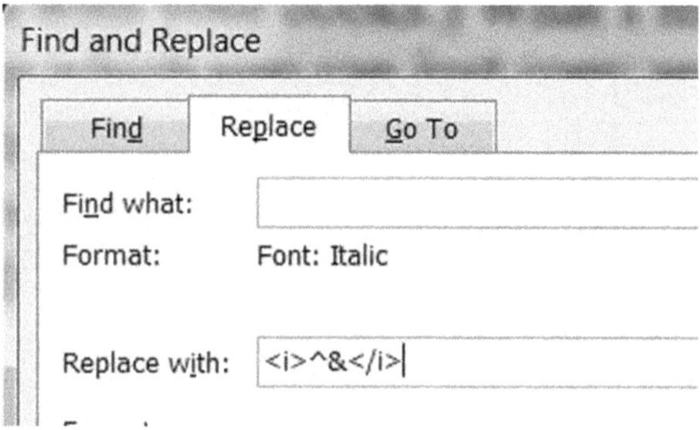
Find and Replace
Find
Replace
Go To
Find what:
Format:
Font: Italic
Replace with:
<i>^&</i>

Pic. 10b

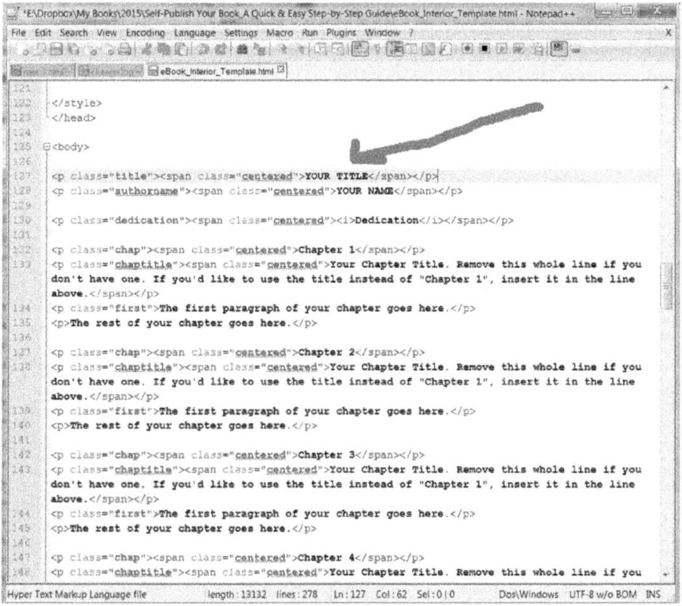


```
</style>
</head>

<body>

<p class="title"><span class="centered">YOUR TITLE</span></p>
<p class="authorname"><span class="centered">YOUR NAME</span></p>

<p class="dedication"><span class="centered"><i>Dedication</i></span></p>

<p class="chap"><span class="centered">Chapter 1</span></p>
<p class="chaptitle"><span class="centered">Your Chapter Title. Remove this whole line if you don't have one. If you'd like to use the title instead of "Chapter 1", insert it in the line above.</span></p>
<p class="first">The first paragraph of your chapter goes here.</p>
<p>The rest of your chapter goes here.</p>

<p class="chap"><span class="centered">Chapter 2</span></p>
<p class="chaptitle"><span class="centered">Your Chapter Title. Remove this whole line if you don't have one. If you'd like to use the title instead of "Chapter 1", insert it in the line above.</span></p>
<p class="first">The first paragraph of your chapter goes here.</p>
<p>The rest of your chapter goes here.</p>

<p class="chap"><span class="centered">Chapter 3</span></p>
<p class="chaptitle"><span class="centered">Your Chapter Title. Remove this whole line if you don't have one. If you'd like to use the title instead of "Chapter 1", insert it in the line above.</span></p>
<p class="first">The first paragraph of your chapter goes here.</p>
<p>The rest of your chapter goes here.</p>

<p class="chap"><span class="centered">Chapter 4</span></p>
<p class="chaptitle"><span class="centered">Your Chapter Title. Remove this whole line if you
```

Pic. 10c

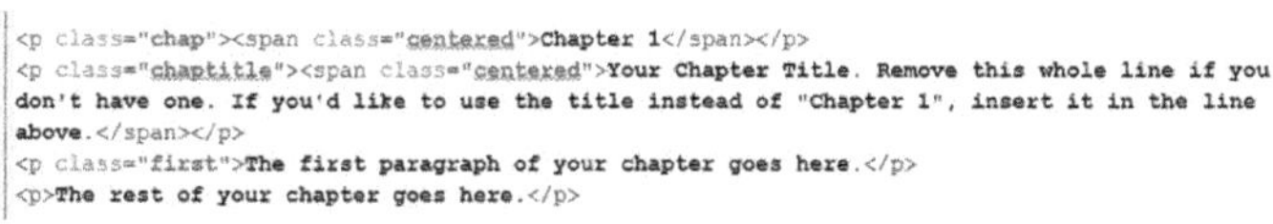

```
<p class="chap"><span class="centered">Chapter 1</span></p>
<p class="chaptitle"><span class="centered">Your Chapter Title. Remove this whole line if you don't have one. If you'd like to use the title instead of "Chapter 1", insert it in the line above.</span></p>
<p class="first">The first paragraph of your chapter goes here.</p>
<p>The rest of your chapter goes here.</p>
```

Pic. 10d

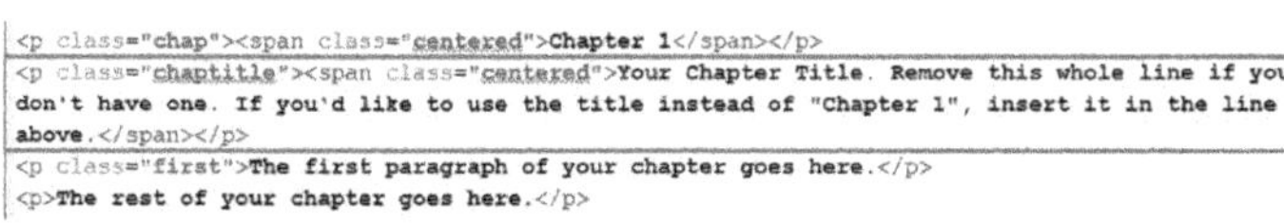

```
<p class="chap"><span class="centered">Chapter 1</span></p>
<p class="chaptitle"><span class="centered">Your Chapter Title. Remove this whole line if you don't have one. If you'd like to use the title instead of "Chapter 1", insert it in the line above.</span></p>
<p class="first">The first paragraph of your chapter goes here.</p>
<p>The rest of your chapter goes here.</p>
```

Pic. 10e

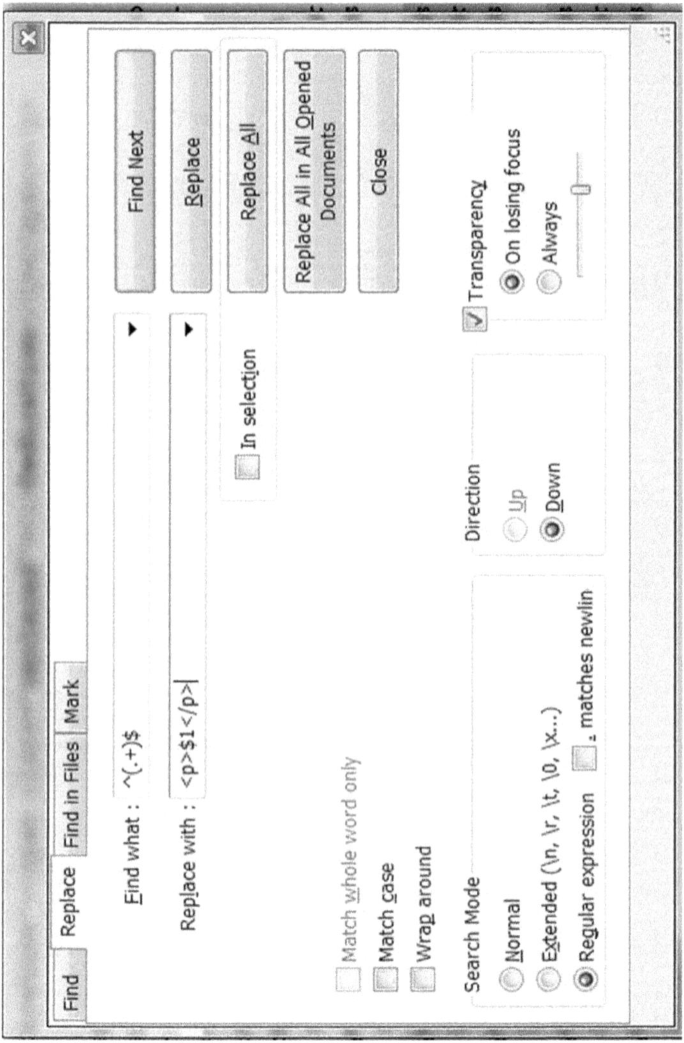
Find
Replace
Find in Files
Mark
Find what : ^(.+)$
Replace with : <p>$1</p>
Find Next
Replace
In selection
Replace All
Replace All in All Opened Documents
Close
Match whole word only
Match case
Wrap around
Search Mode
Normal
Extended (\n, \r, \t, \0, \x...)
Regular expression
. matches newlin
Direction
Up
Down
Transparency
On losing focus
Always

Pic. 10f

```
<body>

<p class="title"><span class="centered">YOUR TITLE</span></p>
<p class="authorname"><span class="centered">YOUR NAME</span></p>

<p class="dedication"><span class="centered"><i>Dedication</i></span></p>

<p class="chap"><span class="centered">Chapter 1</span></p>
<p class="chaptitle"><span class="centered">Your Chapter Title. Remove this whole line if you
don't have one. If you'd like to use the title instead of "Chapter 1", insert it in the line
above.</span></p>
<p class="first">The first paragraph of your chapter goes here.</p>
<p>The rest of your chapter goes here. The rest of your chapter goes here. The rest of your
chapter goes here. The rest of your chapter goes here. The rest of your chapter goes here.
The rest of your chapter goes here. The rest of your chapter goes here. The rest of your
chapter goes here.</p>
<p>The rest of your chapter goes here. The rest of your chapter goes here. The rest of your
chapter goes here. The rest of your chapter goes here. The rest of your chapter goes here.
The rest of your chapter goes here. The rest of your chapter goes here. The rest of your
chapter goes here.</p>
<p>The rest of your chapter goes here. The rest of your chapter goes here. The rest of your
chapter goes here. The rest of your chapter goes here. The rest of your chapter goes here.
The rest of your chapter goes here. The rest of your chapter goes here. The rest of your
chapter goes here.</p>
<p>The rest of your chapter goes here. The rest of your chapter goes here. The rest of your
chapter goes here. The rest of your chapter goes here. The rest of your chapter goes here.
The rest of your chapter goes here. The rest of your chapter goes here. The rest of your
chapter goes here.</p>
```

Pic. 10g

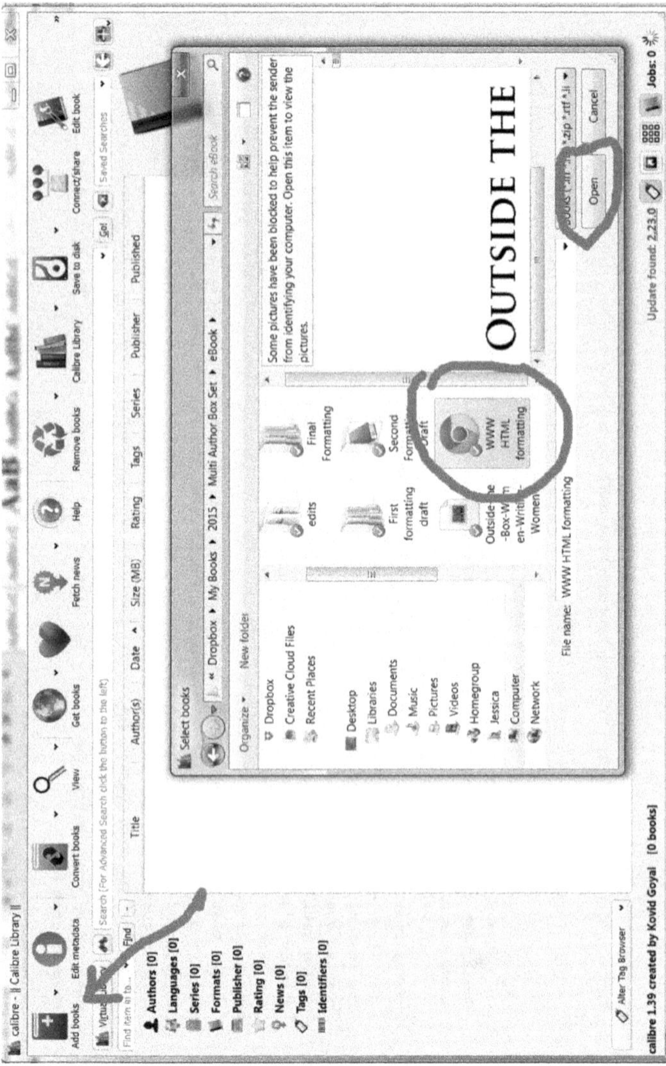
calibre - || Calibre Library ||
Add books
Edit metadata
Convert books
View
Get books
Fetch news
Help
Remove books
Calibre Library
Save to disk
Connect/share
Edit book
Title
Author(s)
Date
Size (MB)
Rating
Tags
Series
Publisher
Published
Authors [0]
Languages [0]
Series [0]
Formats [0]
Publisher [0]
Rating [0]
News [0]
Tags [0]
Identifiers [0]
Select books
Dropbox ▸ My Books ▸ 2015 ▸ Multi Author Box Set ▸ eBook ▸
Organize ▾
New folder
Dropbox
Creative Cloud Files
Recent Places
Desktop
Libraries
Documents
Music
Pictures
Videos
Homegroup
Jessica
Computer
Network
edits
Final Formatting
First formatting draft
Second Formatting Draft
WWW HTML formatting
Some pictures have been blocked to help prevent the sender from identifying your computer. Open this item to view the pictures.
OUTSIDE THE
File name: WWW HTML formatting
Open
Cancel
calibre 1.39 created by Kovid Goyal [0 books]
Update found: 2.23.0
Jobs: 0

Pic. 11a

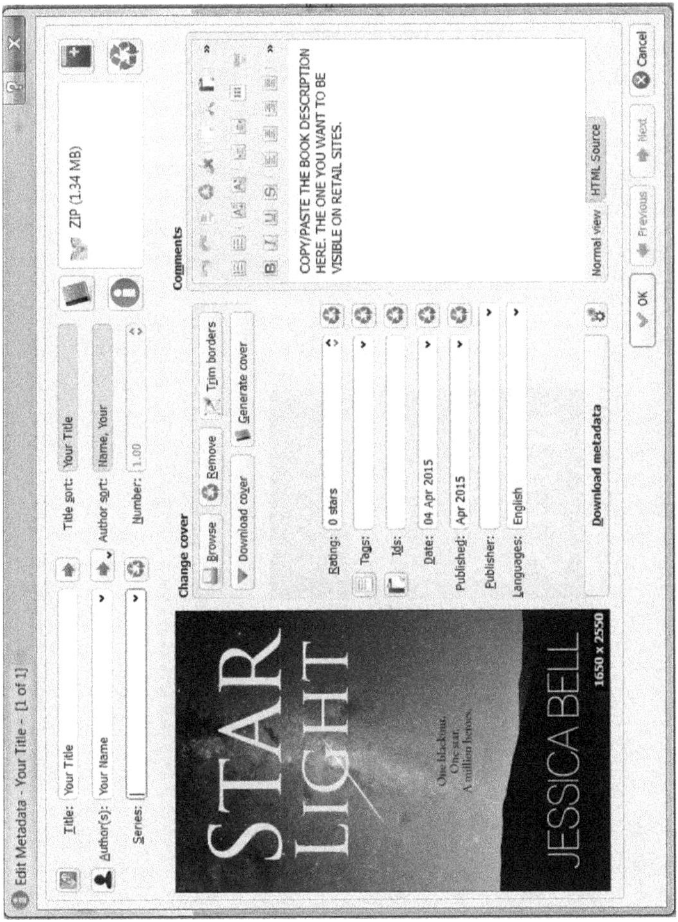
Edit Metadata - Your Title - [1 of 1]
Title: Your Title
Title sort: Your Title
Author(s): Your Name
Author sort: Name, Your
Series:
Number: 1.00
ZIP (1.34 MB)
Change cover
Browse
Remove
Trim borders
Download cover
Generate cover
Rating: 0 stars
Tags:
Ids:
Date: 04 Apr 2015
Published: Apr 2015
Publisher:
Languages: English
Download metadata
Comments
COPY/PASTE THE BOOK DESCRIPTION HERE. THE ONE YOU WANT TO BE VISIBLE ON RETAIL SITES.
Normal view
HTML Source
OK
Previous
Next
Cancel
STAR LIGHT
One black hair. One star. A million heroes.
JESSICA BELL
1650 x 2550

Pic. 11b

Convert Your Title
Input format: ZIP
Output format: MOBI
EPUB
MOBI
AZW3
FB2
HTMLZ
LIT
LRF
PDB
PDF
PMLZ
Look & Feel
Heuristic Processing
Page Setup
Structure Detection
Table of Contents
Search & Replace
MOBI Output
Debug
Book Cover
Title: Your Title
Author(s): Your Name
Author Sort: Name, Your
Publisher:
Tags:
Series:
Book 1.00
STAR LIGHT
JESSICA BELL
COPY/PASTE THE BOOK DESCRIPTION HERE. THE ONE YOU WANT TO BE VISIBLE ON RETAIL SITES.
Change cover image:
Use cover from source file
Normal view
HTML Source
Change the title of this book
Restore Defaults
OK
Cancel

Pic. 11c

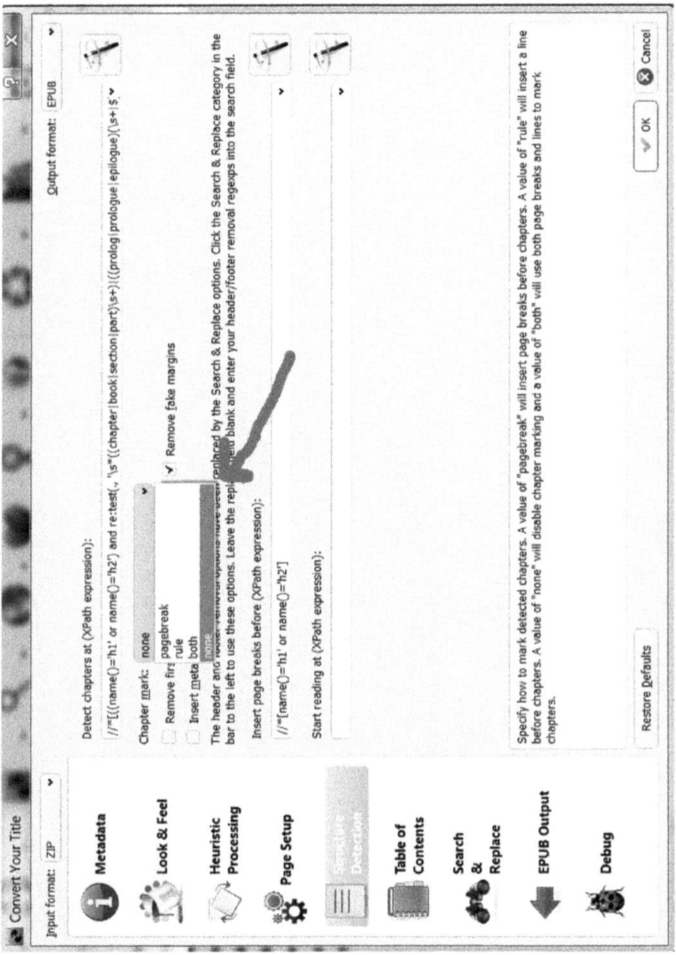
Convert Your Title
Input format: ZIP
Output format: EPUB
Metadata
Look & Feel
Heuristic Processing
Page Setup
Structure Detection
Table of Contents
Search & Replace
EPUB Output
Debug
Detect chapters at (XPath expression):
Chapter mark: none
pagebreak
rule
both
none
Remove fake margins
Insert page breaks before (XPath expression):
//*[name()='h1' or name()='h2']
Start reading at (XPath expression):
Specify how to mark detected chapters. A value of "pagebreak" will insert page breaks before chapters. A value of "rule" will insert a line before chapters. A value of "none" will disable chapter marking and a value of "both" will use both page breaks and lines to mark chapters.
Restore Defaults
OK
Cancel

Pic. 11d

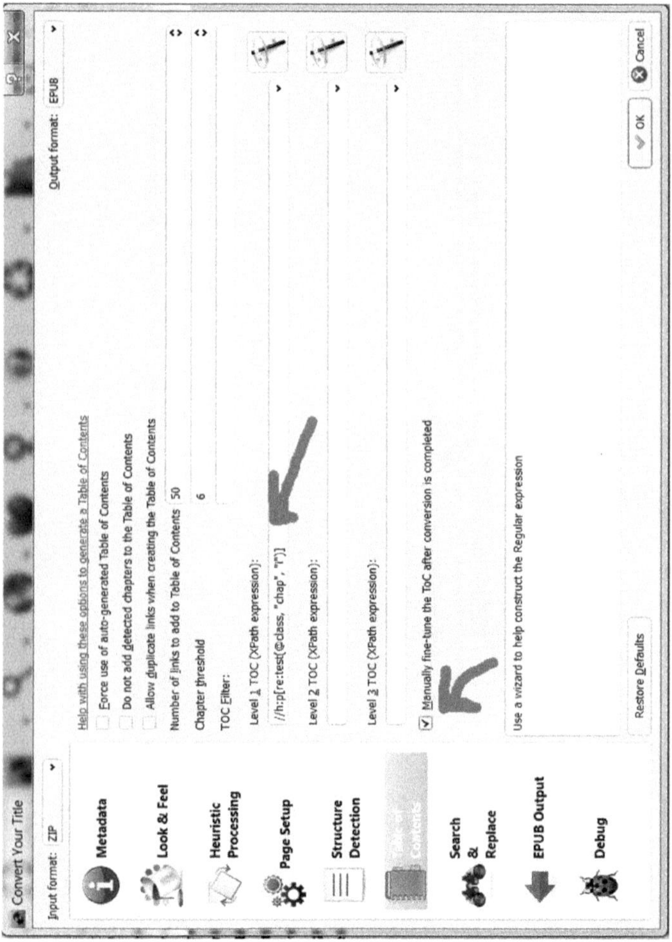
Convert Your Title
Input format: ZIP
Output format: EPUB
Metadata
Look & Feel
Heuristic Processing
Page Setup
Structure Detection
Table of Contents
Search & Replace
EPUB Output
Debug
Help with using these options to generate a Table of Contents
Force use of auto-generated Table of Contents
Do not add detected chapters to the Table of Contents
Allow duplicate links when creating the Table of Contents
Number of links to add to Table of Contents 50
Chapter threshold 6
TOC Filter:
Level 1 TOC (XPath expression):
//h:p[re:test(@class, "chap", "i")]
Level 2 TOC (XPath expression):
Level 3 TOC (XPath expression):
Manually fine-tune the ToC after conversion is completed
Use a wizard to help construct the Regular expression
Restore Defaults
OK
Cancel

Pic. 11e

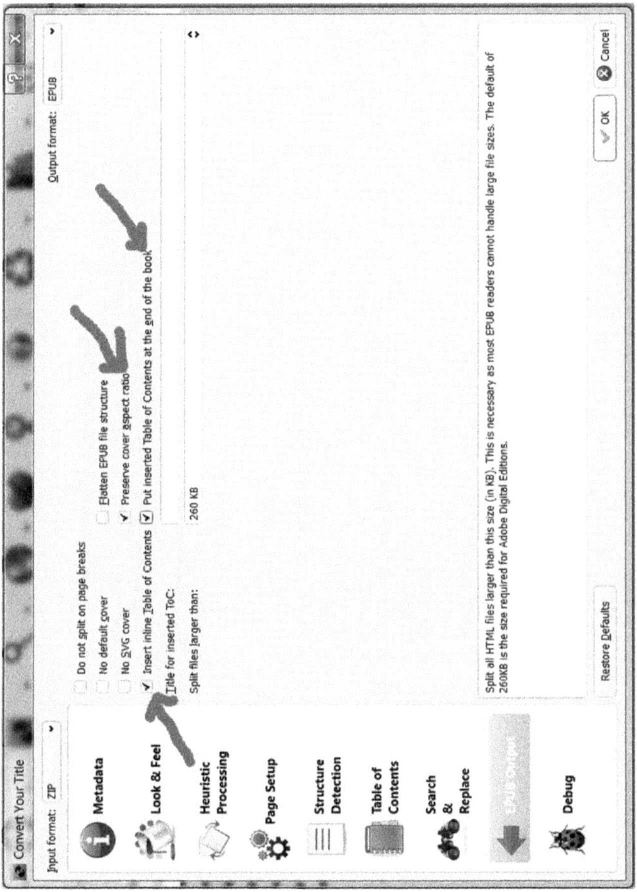
Convert Your Title
Input format: ZIP
Output format: EPUB
Metadata
Look & Feel
Heuristic Processing
Page Setup
Structure Detection
Table of Contents
Search & Replace
Debug
Do not split on page breaks
No default cover
No SVG cover
Insert inline Table of Contents
Title for inserted ToC:
Split files larger than:
Flatten EPUB file structure
Preserve cover aspect ratio
Put inserted Table of Contents at the end of the book
260 KB
Split all HTML files larger than this size (in KB). This is necessary as most EPUB readers cannot handle large file sizes. The default of 260KB is the size required for Adobe Digital Editions.
Restore Defaults
OK
Cancel

Pic. 11f

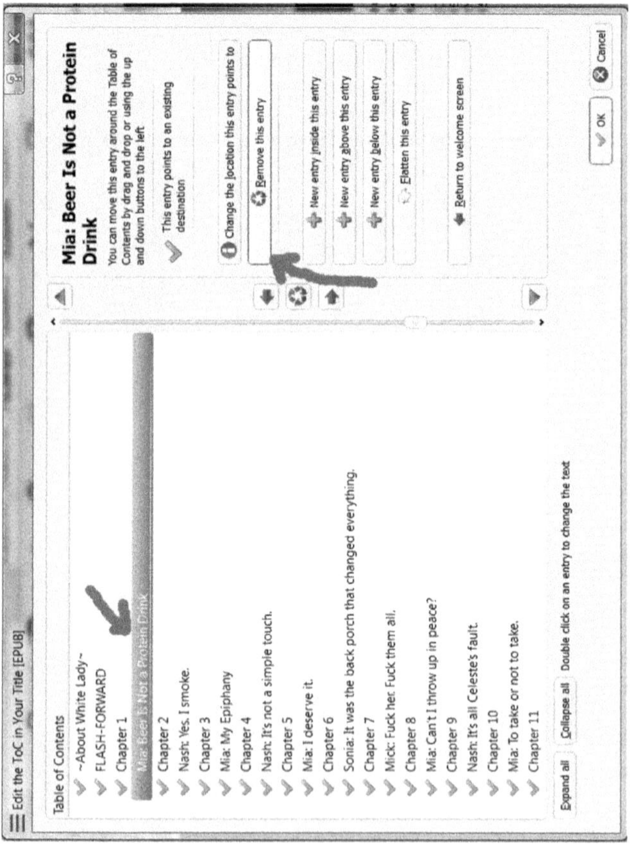

Pic. 11g

Pic. 11h

Lightning Source UK Ltd.
Milton Keynes UK
UKHW02f1822270318
320138UK00015B/283/P

9 780994 283740